Expanding Architecture's Territory in the Design and Delivery of Buildings

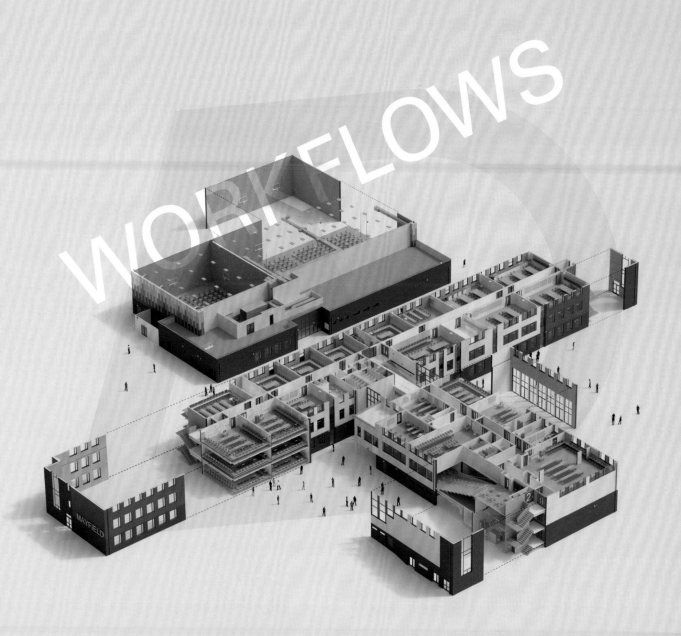

WORKFLOWS

ARCHITECTURAL DESIGN
May/June 2017

Profile
No 247

PLANT –
Atelier Peter Kis,
The Great Rock,
Budapest Zoo &
Botanical Garden,
Budapest,
Hungary,
2012

David Miller Architects,
Refurbishment of the
Media Centre,
Lord's Cricket Ground,
London,
2017

ISSN 0003-8504
ISBN 978-1119-317845

Editorial Offices
John Wiley & Sons
9600 Garsington Road
Oxford
OX4 2DQ

T +44 (0)1865 776868

Consultant Editor
Helen Castle

Managing Editor
Caroline Ellerby
Caroline Ellerby Publishing

Freelance Contributing Editor
Abigail Grater

Publisher
Paul Sayer

Art Direction + Design
CHK Design:
Christian Küsters
Christos Kontogeorgos

Production Editor
Elizabeth Gongde

Prepress
Artmedia, London

Printed in Italy by Printer
Trento Srl

Front and back cover:
Henry Grosman/BanG
studio, Workflows vector
diagram, 2006. © Henry
Grosman/BanG studio

Inside front cover:
Specific Objects,
European Ceramic
Workcentre. Oisterwijk,
The Netherlands,
2016. © Rhett Russo

03/2017

FSC
MIX
Paper from
responsible sources
www.fsc.org   FSC® C015829

△D   ARCHITECTURAL DESIGN

May/June	Profile No.
2017	**247**

Disclaimer
The Publisher and Editors cannot be held responsible
for errors or any consequences arising from the use
of information contained in this journal; the views and
opinions expressed do not necessarily reflect those of
the Publisher and Editors, neither does the publication
of advertisements constitute any endorsement by
the Publisher and Editors of the products advertised.

Journal Customer Services
For ordering information,
claims and any enquiry
concerning your journal
subscription please go to
www.wileycustomerhelp
.com/ask or contact your
nearest office.

Americas
E: cs-journals@wiley.com
T: +1 781 388 8598 or
+1 800 835 6770 (toll free
in the USA & Canada)

**Europe, Middle East
and Africa**
E: cs-journals@wiley.com
T: +44 (0)1865 778315

Asia Pacific
E: cs-journals@wiley.com
T: +65 6511 8000

Japan (for Japanese-
speaking support)
E: cs-japan@wiley.com
T: +65 6511 8010 or 005 316
50 480 (toll-free)

Visit our Online Customer
Help available in 7 languages
at www.wileycustomerhelp
.com/ask

Print ISSN: 0003-8504
Online ISSN: 1554-2769

Prices are for six issues
and include postage and
handling charges. Individual-
rate subscriptions must be
paid by personal cheque or
credit card. Individual-rate
subscriptions may not be
resold or used as library
copies.

All prices are subject to
change without notice.

Identification Statement
Periodicals Postage paid
at Rahway, NJ 07065.
Air freight and mailing in
the USA by Mercury Media
Processing, 1850 Elizabeth
Avenue, Suite C, Rahway,
NJ 07065, USA.

USA Postmaster
Please send address changes
to *Architectural Design*,
John Wiley & Sons Inc.,
c/o The Sheridan Press,
PO Box 465, Hanover,
PA 17331, USA

Rights and Permissions
Requests to the Publisher
should be addressed to:
Permissions Department
John Wiley & Sons Ltd
The Atrium
Southern Gate
Chichester
West Sussex PO19 8SQ
UK

F: +44 (0)1243 770 620
E: Permissions@wiley.com

Subscribe to △D
△D is published bimonthly
and is available to purchase
on both a subscription basis
and as individual volumes
at the following prices.

Prices
Individual copies:
£24.99 / US$39.95
Individual issues on
△D App for iPad:
£9.99 / US$13.99
Mailing fees for print
may apply

Annual Subscription Rates
Student: £84 / US$129
print only
Personal: £128 / US$201
print and iPad access
Institutional: £275 / US$516
print or online
Institutional: £330 / US$620
combined print and online
6-issue subscription on
△D App for iPad: £44.99 /
US$64.99

Richard Garber is a partner at the award-winning New York-based firm GRO Architects. In his work, he utilises technology as it relates to formal speculation, simulation, manufacturing and building delivery to generate innovative design, assembly and construction solutions. He is the author of *BIM Design: Realising the Creative Potential of Building Information Modeling* (John Wiley & Sons, 2014), and Guest-Editor of △ *Closing the Gap: Information Models in Contemporary Design Practice* (March/April 2009). Both publications examine the capacity of design computing and building information modelling (BIM) to augment design-side operations, as opposed to simply making them more efficient. This led to the idea of architectural workflows, and their ability to expand the territory in which architects operate.

Garber has taught and lectured on design and technology internationally, most recently at the New Jersey Institute of Technology (NJIT). He holds a Bachelor of Architecture from Rensselaer Polytechnic Institute in New York, and a Master of Science in Advanced Architectural Design from Columbia University's Graduate School of Architecture, Planning and Preservation (GSAPP). The December 2010 issue of *Dwell* magazine named him as one of the 32 new faces of design, and showcased his precast concrete housing prototype PREttyFAB.

Over the last 15 years, he has been involved in numerous projects that have been acclaimed as novel for their design and delivery. As a designer at SHoP Architects he was involved in early projects such as A-Wall (2000) and Dunescape at MoMA PS-1 (2001) in New York. SHoP has since applied the design methods and workflows developed for these to larger-scale projects, including the Han Gil Sa Book House in Seoul (2002–03) for which Garber was project manager. At GRO he has developed workflows that link material systems such as precast concrete and modular construction to building projects during the design, pre-construction and construction phases. These include PREttyFAB (2009), for which a workflow with a precast concrete fabricator was imagined, and the Jackson Green affordable housing (2014) in Jersey City, New Jersey, for which a workflow engaging a modular construction company was devised.

His recent work engages the increasing influence of ecological thought on architecture, and has yielded planning projects in the US and China, including Zhangdu Lake Farm, a new community in the Chinese countryside designed to incorporate ecologically sustainable infrastructure. The project received the Bronze Medal for Excellence in Planning from the City of Wuhan, Hubei Province. In addition to his work with SHoP, he was designer at Greg Lynn FORM on the Korean Presbyterian Church of New York (1999).

DIGITAL WORKFLOWS AND THE EXPANDED TERRITORY OF THE ARCHITECT

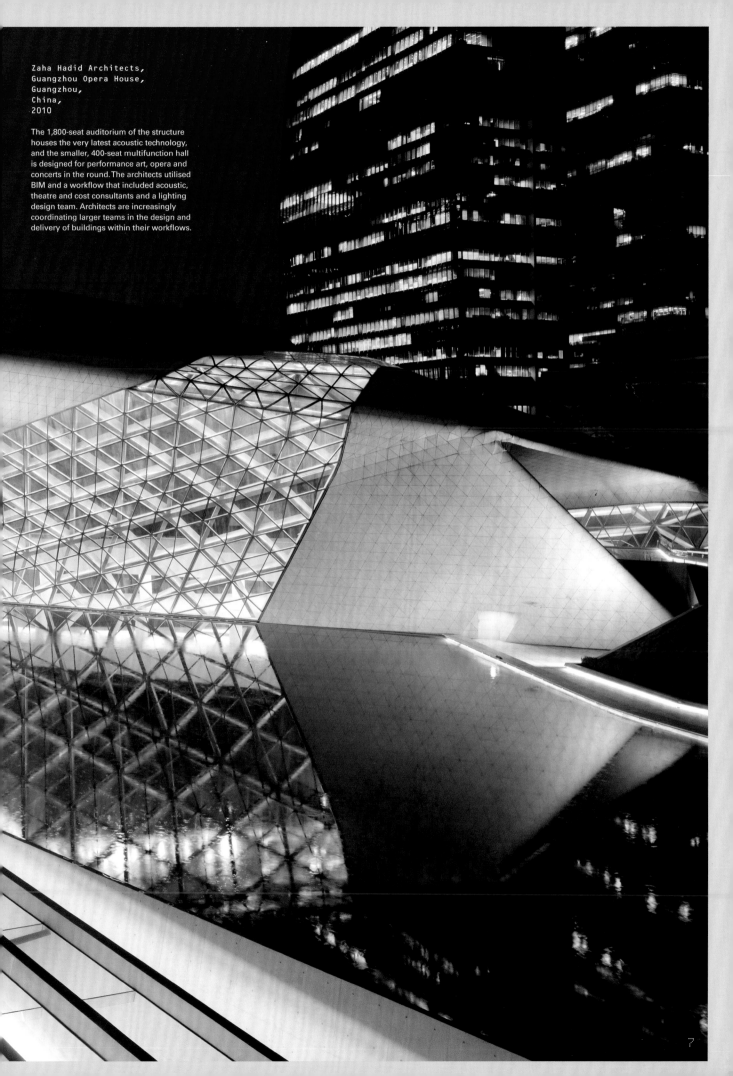

Zaha Hadid Architects,
Guangzhou Opera House,
Guangzhou,
China,
2010

The 1,800-seat auditorium of the structure houses the very latest acoustic technology, and the smaller, 400-seat multifunction hall is designed for performance art, opera and concerts in the round. The architects utilised BIM and a workflow that included acoustic, theatre and cost consultants and a lighting design team. Architects are increasingly coordinating larger teams in the design and delivery of buildings within their workflows.

The synthesis of building information modelling (BIM) platforms with digital simulation and increasing access to data in the form of building performance has allowed contemporary architects to develop workflows in collaboration with others in the design and construction process. Beyond design intent and process, workflows now occupy an expanded territory within architectural practice, merging digital design operations with construction activities, project delivery, and post-occupation scenarios in both virtual and actual formats.

WORKFLOW ORIGINS

In current business practice, a workflow is defined as a 'progression of steps (tasks, events, interactions) that comprise a work process, involve two or more persons, and create or add value to the organization's activities'.[1] However, workflows date back to the industrial processes developed in the 18th century. In their book *Workflow Modeling* (2008), Alec Sharp and Patrick McDermott illustrate the need for workflow design by tracing the demise of the role of craftworkers, 'highly skilled people like weavers, blacksmiths, or jewelers who were responsible for all phases of making a complete, finished product'.[2] With the development of James Watt's steam engine in 1781, they suggest, as manufacturing processes and products became more complex, the work of such artisans was instead divided among teams of workers, each performing a specialised task. Specialisation led to a huge increase in the number of products that could be produced. However, the 'real legacy' of the Industrial Revolution was not any individual product, such as the steam engine, but the idea that complex work could be subdivided into more simple tasks.[3]

At the start of the 20th century, advances in manufacturing technology such as the Fordist assembly line made mass production and mass consumption possible, at the same time revealing that the specialists who worked the line in fact needed no special skills at all – they simply needed to be trained how to repeat a particular task. By the 1950s the term 'workflow' was already being used in office management systems, taking hold in the 1990s with the widespread adoption of information technologies in business and manufacturing practices.[4]

Sharp and McDermott see this shift as a 'reengineering' of work processes: 'Measurement would shift from individual tasks … to the achievement of value … The innovative use of information technology was a crucial factor, but so was rethinking the *flow of work*, the measurements that motivated performance, the underlying policies of the enterprise, and other enabling factors.'[5] It is useful to think about such processes as part of the design and delivery of buildings – two equally important yet sometimes opposing aspects of architects' work that have not always enjoyed a seamless transition.

RE-ENGINEERING THE 1990S

As a way of positioning the divide, I recall an exchange that occurred when I was a graduate student at Columbia University in New York in the late 1990s with the then Dean James Polshek. At that time, students were being introduced to state-of-the-art software packages to be utilised in the design of their projects. While these were inherently parametric – they could be numerically driven as well as employed as more standard 3D modelling tools – the ability to understand a proposed design's impact on a site, or the functional or performative relationship of its architectural componentry, were not yet achievable. Accordingly, such tools quickly drew criticism from a group of malcontents who posited that architects were in essence using them simply to advance their interest in novel architectural formalism.

Though generally complimentary about my formal variation and embracing of the new tools available to Columbia students, Dean Polshek's commentary took a turn when he said: 'But you made a building.' This criticism caught me off guard, not least because I had specifically gone to graduate school to design buildings, but more importantly because he seemed to suggest that these novel tools did not really have a place in the making of real architecture. Even back then, in the midst of what has since become characterised as the 'digital turn',[6] myself and likeminded colleagues were very interested in devising ways to move geometric data through different analogue and digital processes, a precursor to the more robust workflows described in this issue of ⌂, to propose building designs that were measurable and, ultimately, constructible.

My exchange with Dean Polshek really spoke to the emerging divide between those who embraced a more traditional way of designing and constructing buildings, and those of us who believed in something new that would give way some years later to the BIM systems that revolutionised the way we design and build today. In the late 1990s, this computer-driven geometric project was truly experimental in terms of formal exploration, but led to a sort of excess in geometry that was seen as disconnected from a social agenda. Simpler geometric configurations that could be more readily understood by the masses were the preferred option; and it seemed impossible that an architect might give equal attention to complex formal strategies while simultaneously addressing the complexities of social problems at the time.

The idea of formal exploration was seen as a kind of esoteric practice on the fringes of architectural design, detached from the social objectives of the broad profession. Still, these computing adventures would eventually lead to advances in how architects design buildings and communicate with others, as witnessed in the early collaborations between SHoP Architects and Buro Happold Consulting Engineers, such as the Porter House in New York City (2003), and the Carousel (2001) and Camera Obscura (2005), both at Mitchell Park in Greenport,

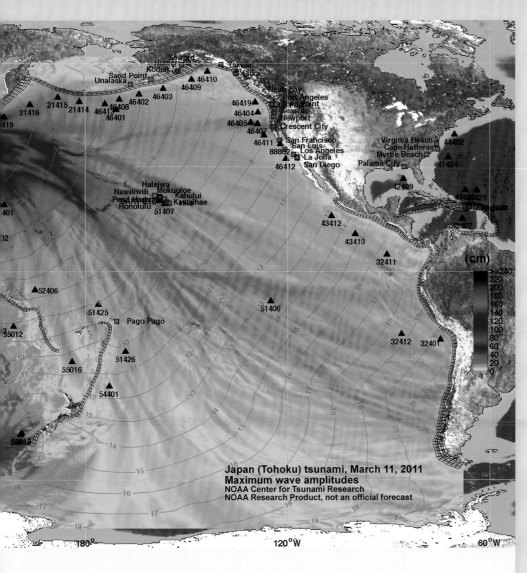

National Oceanic and
Atmospheric Administration
(NOAA),
Tsunami Energy Map,
Japan,
11 March 2011

Advances in visual and information
technology, and its management, have
enabled the design of new and innovative
workflows. The NOAA's Center for Tsunami
Research produced this graphic of wave
energy in the Pacific Ocean following the
2011 earthquakes in Japan.

Japan (Tohoku) tsunami, March 11, 2011
Maximum wave amplitudes
NOAA Center for Tsunami Research
NOAA Research Product, not an official forecast

(cm)

In current business practice, a workflow is defined as
a 'progression of steps (tasks, events, interactions) that
comprise a work process, involve two or more persons,
and create or add value to the organization's activities'.

Plane factory assembly line,
England,
c 1900

This factory, somewhere in England,
shows a floor filled with spitfire fighters
in the making. It is quite similar to
how US assembly lines at the time
were organised, however in England
it was not the planes themselves that
moved, but rather the workmen. This
seems to challenge the Fordist idea that
unskilled workers repeat the same task
continuously.

GRO Architects,
Academy Street
Micro-Housing,
Jersey City,
New Jersey,
2015

BIM suites such as Autodesk's Revit are used by architects to virtually construct a building prior to actual construction. GRO's micro-housing proposal imagines 18.5-square-metre (200-square-foot) fully furnished living units that need to be outfitted with all of the amenities of a more typically sized apartment. The Revit model was shared not only across the design and engineering team, but was also crucial for subcontractors such as plumbers and electricians to understand their scope of work within a very small space.

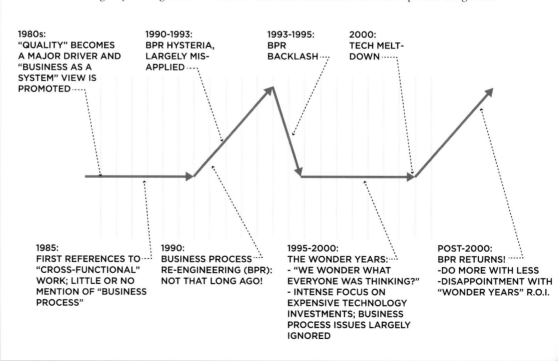

New York.[7] On this point, professor and practising architect Scott Marble has written: 'the impact that this work had on the development in industry has become the foundation for new design approaches that are more responsive to, and even inspired by, the possibilities of digital fabrication techniques.'[8]

FEEDBACK AND THE FLOW OF WORK

Ultimately, the workflows architects and designers use today have shifted from the more linear processes of the assembly lines of the 20th century to those that allow for feedback across the design team and project timescale. The adoption of BIM has enabled new workflows that are more iterative and collaborative, and more than ever coordinated with the downstream processes of manufacturing and building delivery. This idea, that an architectural workflow can encompass pre-construction design activities, construction phases and, ultimately, the occupation of a building, moves the discussion of a design process to one that is more broad and defined by and with collaborators across the architectural, engineering and construction (AEC) spectrum. Process is no longer an explicitly design-side operation; architects are increasingly involved in component manufacturing and construction, allowing them to expand the territory and traditional role in building design they have held since the time of Leon Battista Alberti in the 15th century.[9]

Workflows, in fact, are a kind of hidden phenomenon in completed buildings. Buildings alone, especially complex ones, cannot convey the collaborative activities that design teams have developed in the service of construction execution. Though in many instances designed by architects, workflows are participatory, engaging engineers, fabrications, contractors and others within the building delivery process. This issue of ⅅ demonstrates the importance of adopting virtual-to-actual workflows in contemporary architectural design by linking access to various data and material flows with specific design and

GRO Architects,
The rise and fall of continuous process development,
2016

In their book *Workflow Modeling* (2008), in a graphic referred to as the 'rise and fall of continuous process development', Alec Sharp and Patrick McDermott trace the role of information technology in refining business workflows from the 1980s through to today. Analogous technologies were transforming the AEC industry during the same period, with similar missteps.

1980s: "QUALITY" BECOMES A MAJOR DRIVER AND "BUSINESS AS A SYSTEM" VIEW IS PROMOTED

1990-1993: BPR HYSTERIA, LARGELY MIS-APPLIED

1993-1995: BPR BACKLASH

2000: TECH MELT-DOWN

1985: FIRST REFERENCES TO "CROSS-FUNCTIONAL" WORK; LITTLE OR NO MENTION OF "BUSINESS PROCESS"

1990: BUSINESS PROCESS RE-ENGINEERING (BPR): NOT THAT LONG AGO!

1995-2000: THE WONDER YEARS:
- "WE WONDER WHAT EVERYONE WAS THINKING?"
- INTENSE FOCUS ON EXPENSIVE TECHNOLOGY INVESTMENTS; BUSINESS PROCESS ISSUES LARGELY IGNORED

POST-2000: BPR RETURNS!
- DO MORE WITH LESS
- DISAPPOINTMENT WITH "WONDER YEARS" R.O.I.

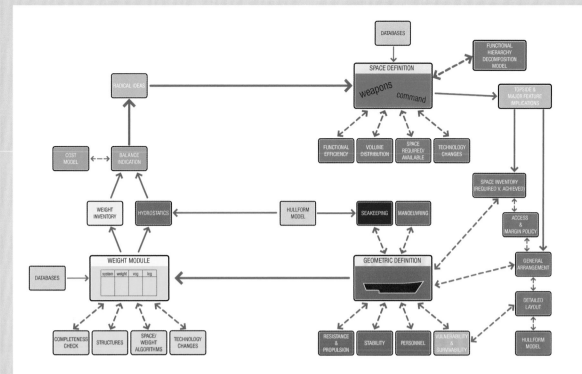

GRO Architects,
Design building
block,
2012

The 'design building block' method for ship design and construction, as developed by DJ Andrews and others. Here, the different parts are developed at the onset of a digital design process and iterated through simulation and analysis both discretely and as an assembly. The building block represents a fully integrated workflow from initial design to final production.

production techniques, and exposing how both small and larger practices are leveraging digital technologies in novel and efficient ways of delivering increasingly complex building projects. It also looks at how logistics and systemic organisation in related fields such as manufacturing and retail are influencing the way architects approach design problems.

For Scott Marble, the 'logics of digital workflows in architecture have begun to structure the way that architects design, the way that builders build, and the way that industry is reorganizing'.[10] The design of workflows and their value in the actualisation of large and complex building projects has followed the more robust adoption of BIM platforms as well as the idea of integrated project delivery (IPD), both the results of an expanded interest in 3D modelling made possible by advances in computing some 30 years ago. Writing in 2015, Randall Newton, a principal analyst at design industry and business consultants Consilia Vektor, pointed out that more recent developments in information technology and collaborative online environments have made it clear that the 'processes that became standard before the arrival of computers cannot support a fully digital, fully 3D, fully collaborative construction project'.[11] Through BIM, however, much greater degrees of collaboration, efficiency and coordination are possible in operations including costing, fabrication and virtual construction. Yet some sectors of the AEC industry have been slow to adopt these tools.

GRO Architects,
Design workflow
with feedback,
2012

Design workflows in other industries have been developed with a highly articulated relationship between modelling, simulation, prototyping and, ultimately, production. In such a workflow, the linear design and production process shifts to one that is more iterative and allows for feedback from all team members.

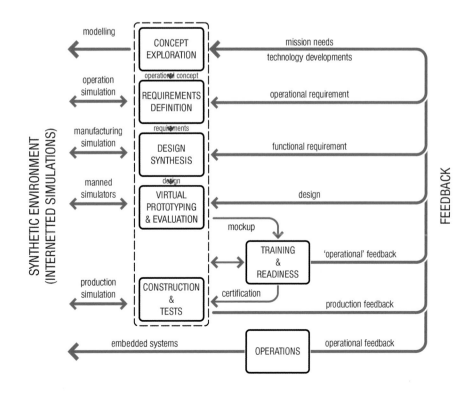

SHoP Architects,
Camera Obscura,
Mitchell Park,
Greenport,
New York,
2005

SHoP's Camera Obscura was an early experiment in direct-to-manufacture construction. The building was modelled entirely in Rhino 3D and rationalised for digital data transfer to manufacturers who produced its components, primarily from laser-cut sheet steel. The project represents a shift from the mass production to the mass customisation of architectural componentry.

BIM CULTURE

Many architects, though, have embraced such objectives, through a more nuanced and developed relationship between architectural design and current technologies. Mass production, for instance, has given way to mass customisation, where instead of people working linearly on an assembly line to produce a single part, the workflow involves a smaller group of workers with some specialised knowledge who can program hardware to variably produce multiple parts. Current workflows thus allow for more bespoke solutions that can be tailored to specific building performance needs. How this differs from the 1990s is in the design team's ability to develop a building scheme that engages various criteria including form, performance, material and energy use, and cost using 3D modelling and simulation tools. Design decisions such as siting and orientation, bulk considerations and accessibility can now be controlled very early in the design process and linked to downstream activities such as material selection and the fabrication of structural or architectural components. Whereas formal variation could always be numerically controlled, it can now be directly connected to the highly specific criteria that creatively drive design decisions.

The increasing use of social media over the last decade has also led to a more widespread international adoption of BIM culture. Passionate about sharing developments, BIM users publish their knowledge and lessons learned through blogs and Twitter. Organisations such as SmartGeometry and the Association for Computer Aided Design in Architecture (ACADIA) also disseminate this thinking across academia and practice. Architects are no longer unwilling, as previously, to share their knowledge with others in the field, and many digital workflows are now explained via YouTube tutorials and described in publications such as Dominik Holzer's *The BIM Manager's Handbook* (2016).[12]

WORKFLOWS AND ARCHITECTURAL PRODUCTION

In a recent white paper published by Autodesk, Lance Parve, a hydrogeologist with the Wisconsin Department of Transportation, speaks of creating 'cross-generational training' opportunities within firms, with 'younger, less-experienced staff working alongside … senior people who don't have … familiarity with parametric modeling tools. The shift offers the impetus for a cultural boost within the organization, with opportunities for mentoring and instilling the firm's values and expertise within the next generation, while taking advantage of the newer skill set.'[13] In their 'From Pencils to Partners' article in this issue of ⊿ (pp 74–81), Autodesk's Ian Keough and Anthony Hauck outline new online environments in which workflows exist that enable such training and collaboration, and facilitate a more horizontal organisation of the design firms themselves.

Design decisions such as siting and orientation, bulk considerations and accessibility can now be controlled very early in the design process

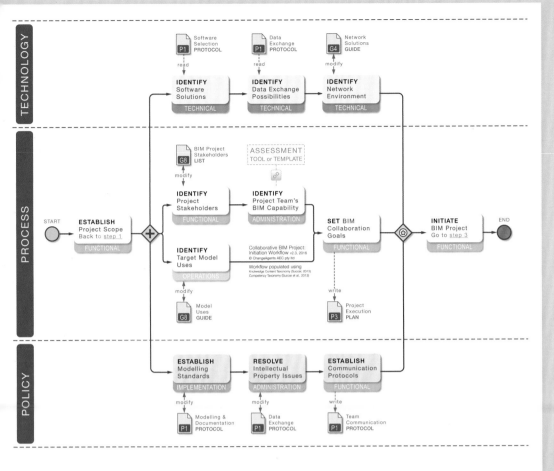

Bilal Succar/Change Agents AEC, Collaborative BIM project initiation workflow, 2016

BIM assessment firm Change Agents AEC helps design firms build BIM competency. Its project initiation workflow merges modelling and data exchange standards, and project scope, across a collaborative and shared environment.

Notes
1. See www.businessdictionary.com/definition/workflow.html.
2. Alec Sharp and Patrick McDermott, 'A Brief History – How the Enterprise Came to Be Process Oriented', *Workflow Modeling: Tools for Process Improvement and Application Development*, Artech House (Boston, MA), 2008, p 16.
3. *Ibid*, p 19.
4. See http://macsparky.com/blog/2013/4/history-of-workflow.
5. Sharp and McDermott, *op cit*, p 23.
6. Mario Carpo (ed), *The Digital Turn in Architecture 1992–2012*, John Wiley & Sons (Chichester), 2013.
7. SHoP/Sharples Holden Pasquarelli, 𝝙 *Versioning: Evolutionary Techniques in Architecture*, Jan/Feb (no 1), 2003.
8. Scott Marble (ed), 'From Process to Workflow: Designing Design, Designing Assembly, Designing Industry', *Digital Workflows in Architecture: Design – Assembly – Industry*, Birkhäuser (Basel), 2012, p 8.
9. See Richard Garber, 'Alberti's Paradigm', in 𝝙 *Closing the Gap: Information Models in Contemporary Design Practice*, March/April (no 2), 2009, p 108.
10. Marble, *op cit*, p 8.
11. See Randal S Newton, 'Bim Workflows are Evolving', *AEC Magazine*, 20 April 2015: http://aecmag.com/59-features/840-bim-workflows-are-evolving.
12. Dominik Holzer, *The BIM Manager's Handbook: Guidance for Professionals in Architecture, Engineering and Construction*, John Wiley & Sons (Chichester), 2001.
13. See www.autodesk.com/solutions/bim/how-to-adopt-bim-workflow-for-civil-projects.

The workflows described in the issue speak broadly to how digital tools have been adopted by architects and engineers and merged with building delivery methods. In her article 'The Fifth Dimension' (pp 28–33), Stacie Wong explains architect-led design–build (ALDB), a form of practice developed by GLUCK+ 'in which the social capital and tacit knowledge of architect and contractor influence the built environment for the better'. In assessing workflows in global practices, Randy Deutsch (pp 56–67) illustrates how prominent architectural firms are engaging in the development of digital workflows to expand both iteration within the design process and direct-to-fabrication potentials in the production of architectural componentry. This is reiterated by Shajay Bhooshan of Zaha Hadid Architects (pp 82–9), where very specific ideas about fabrication can be drive through the development of digital geometry.

Rhett Russo (pp 48–55) and Kutan Ayata (pp 90–95) write about new workflows that merge vector-based geometry with images; and Arup's Seth Wolfe and colleagues (pp 120–27) highlight how technology is changing engineering design operations and leading to further collaboration with architects.

The design of workflows also offers something that critics of digital technologies suggest we have lost: the possibility of bringing a social dimension to the design and delivery of buildings through active stakeholder engagement and participation. In this sense, workflows allow architects to come full circle, by closing the gap between those who have argued that architecture is primarily a social project, and those who have embraced the technologies that have revolutionised architectural design. Featured projects by SHoP Architects (pp 110–12) and GRO Architects (pp 112–19) illustrate how the practices are integrating concepts of local inclusion and knowledge transfer within their work. Other works, including the Duke University Marine Laboratory Campus by GLUCK+ (pp 28–33), demonstrate how through workflows architects are involving local communities as both stakeholders and workforce, bridging the gap between the sometimes irreconcilable social and technical dimensions of a building project.

The inclusive nature of workflows means they can accommodate the personalised design processes of architects as well as integrated engineering strategies and collaborative ideas about building delivery. Through the contributions of a group of accomplished architects, engineers and software designers, this issue of 𝝙 attempts to touch on each of these aspects, and to explain how technologically infused workflows will continue to influence 21st-century design practice. 𝝙

Diller Scofidio + Renfro and Gensler,
Roy and Diana Vagelos Graduate
Education Center,
Columbia University,
New York,
2016

Night view illuminating the building's principal design strategy: the 'study cascade', a network of social and study spaces connected by an exposed 14-storey stairway. The interiors of the cascade, designed to facilitate collaboration and team-based learning, vary in size and configuration; opening to south-facing terraces, they also connect to classrooms and laboratories on the tower's north side.

A Return to the Hand-Driven Workflow

ching
Glass

Does digital design constitute a death-knell for drawing? On the contrary, argues **Sean A Gallagher,** Director of Sustainable Design at Diller Scofidio + Renfro. This well-known New York architecture practice retains a strong culture of sketching at all stages, due to its immediacy in recording ideas and its efficiency in communicating them. But the firm's members embrace new technology at the same time. iPads, for instance, offer easy transportability and can capture smooth movements of the hand; while new interfaces can enhance fluidity and allow complex layering.

Architects tend to do their best thinking on planes, trains, and in remote locations in front of a fire with whiskey in hand. We currently live in a mobile digital society imagined by theorists like Richard Buckminister Fuller, who contemplated the potential of the phone and radio to transform everyday life – work and play. By 1930, Fuller was discussing ideas about a near-future global society with universal mobility embracing a digital culture and exploiting every benefit of modern technology. This near future is now, and while it has brought much of the promise imagined, for architects it has also unintentionally constrained certain aspects of our craft and workflow.

Architects communicate by drawing through spatial problems, and our ability to think through these challenges often requires a conversation between our mind and hand to organise our thoughts and critically think through the ideas. This process, grounded in centuries of instinct and practice, began to erode as digital tools evolved in the late 20th century to facilitate both the visualisation and construction documentation of an architectural project. While the digital interface revolutionised architects' ability to interrogate space within a virtual reality, a time lapse developed between the medium being produced to investigate the idea

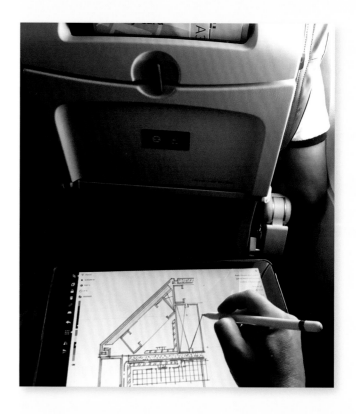

Sean A Gallagher/Diller Scofidio + Renfro, Drafting an exterior wall detail for the University of Chicago Rubenstein Forum project on a plane, 2016

Aeroplanes are great places to focus without distraction and to think through a problem. After meeting with the project's design-assist contractors in Chicago, Gallagher took the time on a return flight to New York to draw through the problem with the meeting conversations fresh in his mind. The ability to draft on glass meant that the initial sketches from the meeting could be translated into a full-scale detail to better interrogate the problem.

and the person who was critically thinking through the design process. As a result, what was gained from digital documentation in terms of speed, precision and editability was at the expense of critical thought at every intersection of the design process.

Currently, 3D modelling platforms are expanding our power to manage, replicate and integrate the informational aspects of an idea. The architecture community's investment in the research and development of building information modelling (BIM) platforms exceeds that expended on the advancement of any previous technology in the history of the profession. And while these new platforms will improve our command over traditional practice and challenge the notion that the architecture, engineering and construction industry underutilise emerging computational technologies, will this investment begin to develop a new digital workflow that restores critical thought at every intersection of the design process?

The underlying promise of the digital interface is more than the management of information, or even the virtual world from which to explore an idea – it is cultural. The notion of working anywhere and everywhere with all the tools necessary to facilitate a discussion with

oneself as well as with one's collaborators will be wildly more powerful within our design workflow than any other computational improvements such as BIM. But the resources the architecture community is devoting to developing enhanced platforms that afford the freedom to work on site, at a consultant's office, or within a place of inspiration are limited. It is in this domain that the sketchbook as an 'everywhere' tool has for centuries proven invaluable to every artist, designer and architect, although the profession has largely ignored it in the shift towards digital interfaces as a primary source of discovery.

Sean A Gallagher/Diller Scofidio + Renfro,
Sketching a sustainability concept diagram
for the Obama Presidential Center competition
while at the Delaware Water Gap,
Montague, New Jersey, 2015

Architects often travel to places of inspiration to think through the specific ideas of a project. The sketchbook, which is limited in scale and versatility, has traditionally served as the tool to critically think through these ideas on site. However, with the ability to draw on glass, the architectural investigation can range in scale as well as in complexity. This concept drawing was drawn at full scale with every stroke type – graphite, marker, sharpie – organised in sheet layers that could be further edited back at the office.

The underlying promise of the digital interface is more than the management of information, or even the virtual world from which to explore an idea – it is cultural.

Sketching as a way of communication is fast and efficient – there is nothing more effective in communicating ideas between two people collaborating on a project than drawing in the presence of one another.

Sketching and the Digital Interface

At Diller Scofidio + Renfro (DS+R) there is a strong culture of sketching to investigate an idea and to determine an approach to a project. This affection for the architect's craft of generations past can be observed through the media released by the studio, often incorporating hand strokes of graphite layered over digital renderings to produce the final image. While it is not unusual for most practices to sketch through their concept designs, the commitment DS+R has to integrating this type of workflow into all phases of design is unique.

Sketching as a way of communication is fast and efficient – there is nothing more effective in communicating ideas between two people collaborating on a project than drawing in the presence of one another. Current digital workflow requires a longer lag time to develop media to express what one is thinking to collaborators than with pencil and paper, and quite often results in loss of momentum and inspiration within the conversation. However, due to the static nature of hand drawings, delivering a project of scale through pencil and paper is currently implausible. Drawing technologies that have the capacity to be more fluid, negotiating the continuous layering of new ideas and additional information throughout the project delivery workflow, have thus dominated the research and development landscape over the last 30 years.

Ricardo Scofidio at his drafting table and Sean A Gallagher with his iPad Pro drafting by hand in the Diller Scofidio + Renfro office, New York, 2016

Fostering a culture of drawing within the office became more difficult as architects' workspaces adapted to the constraints of the mouse, keyboard and monitor. Today, however, touchscreen interfaces afford an opportunity to re-prioritise the workspace to be conducive to drawing while working on digital platforms. Soon there will be no need for a mouse, keyboard or monitor as touchscreen drafting surfaces will accommodate all aspects of architects' current workflow.

But what if the hand sketch were fluid and the paper scaleless? Drawing technologies within the digital realm so far have capitalised most significantly on these two attributes to improve architects' workflow, neither of which precludes the idea of the pencil as the primary source of informational input. In fact, the use of a pencil would have been more intuitive had the digital platform hardware three decades ago bridged the barrier between virtual space and paper. But at that time, the best technology could offer was a point-and-click tool to navigate virtual space through the movement of a mouse. Today, this is no longer the case.

In 2012, I had adopted the iPad as my primary tool for day-to-day workflows – using it as a notebook, sketchbook and camera, and for office-related communication and documentation. But the limited scale of the touchscreen and beta versions of drawing apps restricted my ability to tackle many of the processes associated with the craft of our profession, forcing me to juggle between the drafting board, tablet and computer as the design process of a project moved beyond the conceptual phase. However, at the time it proved extremely useful as a way to organise thoughts and have all my research and documentation at my fingertips to build on an idea no matter my location. I used the touchscreen to write, sketch, view 3D models, mark-up drawings and assemble presentations. There was something familiar and intuitive when using my hand on the screen that overshadowed all the burdens and frustrations of working through the compatibility issues associated with emerging software tools.

Tablet technologies for the design process improved over the years and I soon found myself sketching a great deal on the iPad. The design drawings that were initially constrained to concept-level diagrams began to expand into schematic plans, sections and perspectives. And with this improved range of capabilities I began to incorporate hand drawing more and more into my daily workflow as drafting activities could now occur in remote locations. But what was more interesting was that the drawing apps

Sean A Gallagher/Diller Scofidio + Renfro, Architectural plan study for the University of Chicago Rubenstein Forum drawn on the iPad Pro for coordination with the structural engineer, 2016

Hand drawings composed on the touchscreen interface are similar to computer-aided drafting processes and allow for the layering and organisation of various design components as well as the ability to go back and edit or change the properties of each stroke.

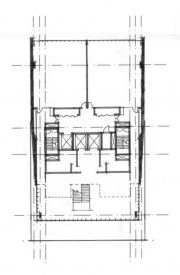

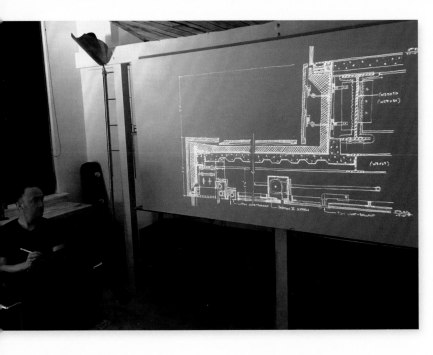

Sean A Gallagher/Diller Scofidio + Renfro, Thinking through a section detail for the Columbia University School of Business Tower on his iPad while simultaneously projecting it on a wall at half scale at his residence in Jersey City, New Jersey, 2014

The touchscreen interface as a paper medium affords the freedom to draft at any scale, and to project in real time the drawing activity at the desired scale for personal investigation or group conversation.

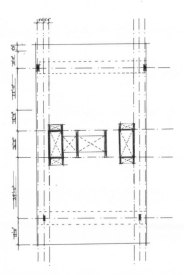

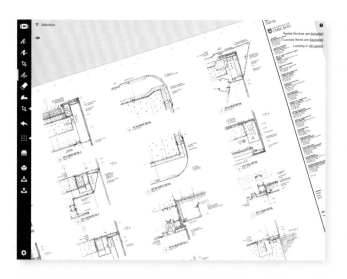

Diller Scofidio + Renfro, University of Chicago
Rubenstein Forum design development drawing set, 2016

The final design development drawing set included coordinated hand-
drawn detailing within the BIM-generated documentation. The details were
hand drawn on the touchscreen interface and could be edited and updated
throughout the design development phase in the drafting views of the BIM
platform.

Sean A Gallagher/Diller Scofidio + Renfro, Exploded
building perspective sketch of exterior wall assembly
options, drawn on the iPad Pro during the University of
Chicago Rubenstein Forum design development phase, 2016

Developing design option media that moves between various scales and
style of drawing to express intent and character can be composed in a single
drawing when using the touchscreen interface. There is no need for post-
production formatting to bring all the pieces together which greatly increases
the speed at which options can be iterated.

began to afford an ability to fine tune and adjust every
hand stroke with a level of precision and flexibility only
possible in digital space. This changed the static nature of
a sketch by allowing the internal conversation between
hand and mind to continue as the drawing built on those
initial lines with a newfound freedom in the knowledge
that one could go back and further tune those first strokes.
Sketching became nonlinear and more fluid, and I became
more comfortable and aggressive with sketching through
ideas; it improved my craft.

Last year Apple altered its traditional course of
making things smaller, and released the iPad Pro with a
touchscreen interface much larger than previous editions.
The 14-inch (35.5-centimetre) wide screen is slightly larger
than a piece of A4 paper, making it a comfortable scale to
draw on while standing or sitting. More importantly, this
difference in surface area made it possible for schematic-
level drafting and modelling activities performed with
the smaller tablet to grow into serious visualisation and
detailing documentation at any phase of design. This
historic movement to a larger digital interface confirms
there is an understanding that over the next century
the necessity to have everything at your fingertips at all
times will move from personal communication devices
into the domain of professional workflows. Our mobile
digital society is now being moulded by the millennials'
digital culture of work and play in public places through
a ground swell of app development. Yet to accommodate
the sophistication of these emerging apps targeting
professional workflows, the touchscreen devices need to
grow and the tool to input the movements of the hand
requires increased sensitivity and precision.

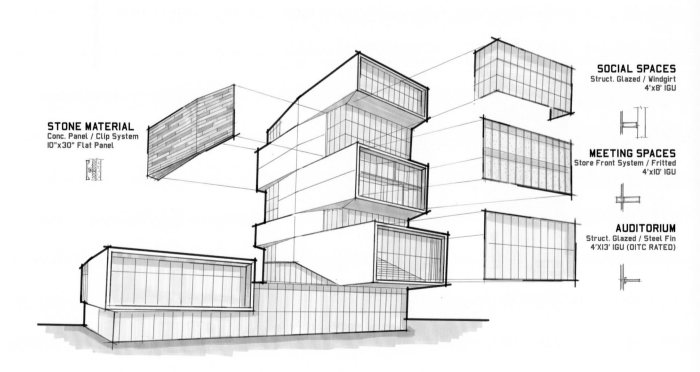

STONE MATERIAL
Conc. Panel / Clip System
10"x30" Flat Panel

SOCIAL SPACES
Struct. Glazed / Windgirt
4'x8' IGU

MEETING SPACES
Store Front System / Fritted
4'x10' IGU

AUDITORIUM
Struct. Glazed / Steel Fin
4'x13' IGU (OITC RATED)

Apple Pencil embraces glass as a drawing medium. It does not attempt to replicate qualities of alternate surfaces more familiar to sketching, or the material thickness of a former drawing utensil. It has an overall weight that fosters a controlled slide across a smooth surface, and a sharp tip to take command of the precision of a virtual interface. The Pencil is a tool that feels familiar in hand and encourages experimentation with the toothless surface of glass. And while glass has previously been a material foreign to drawing activities, its physical properties encourage a fluid movement of hand as well as a layering of visual information. It is only a matter of time before glass will move from a medium that we simply look through, to one that we actively work on; the architecture profession needs to recognise this opportunity.

Collaborating on Glass

Right now there is a real necessity within architects' workflow to sketch on glass. It has become the client's expectation that the profession utilises a project delivery method that implements BIM software, and as a result our day-to-day collaborations with engineers and contractors are regularly facilitated through a shared screen referencing a virtual model of a project's current status. However, while this digital integration process of managing design components fosters a better visual understanding of the issues at hand, the conversation around the virtual table in the effort to move a project forward remains the same: 'Can you sketch that for me?' In the past, a roll of trace and thick sharpie would allow the conversation to continue in a fruitful way, but today the conversation stalls as there is no way to sketch efficiently on the screen, and a follow-up call is required after a sketch visualising the idea is produced in order to move the collaboration forward.

This time lapse in the collaboration process during the design development phases is as destructive to architects' workflow as it is to the inspirational moments of conceptual design. Most BIM and screen-sharing platforms recognise this growing challenge, and have begun to offer mark-up tools as part of their user interfaces. Unfortunately these require the motion of hand and pencil to communicate effectively, and are difficult to control with the unnatural movements of a mouse and pointer. However, BIM and share-screen software companies are quickly expanding into the tablet market and developing app versions of their digital platforms in anticipation of an increased level of remote collaborations within our professional workflow. At DS+R, project collaborations with design consultants and engineers have become more remote over the last five years, and I have now begun to experiment with running coordination meetings from my iPad Pro in order to incorporate the ability to sketch during these conversations. With the touchscreen interface and Apple Pencil, I am able to communicate more effectively with the digital mark-up tools as the discussion navigates the virtual space of the BIM model. And while the ability to sketch is solely at my end, it has greatly improved the collaboration process and restored a more familiar workflow.

Improving Architects' Craft

In truth, hand drawing over 3D model prints has become a natural part of architects' workflow, setting the foundation for a more integrated process between virtual investigations and sketching. The digital equivalent of this is similar, but is greatly improved in terms of speed, precision and editability when utilising a touchscreen interface. More importantly, the design activities carried out by hand have now become a direct part of the digital workflow required to deliver projects of scale in today's marketplace. The emerging capacity to sketch on glass has meant that DS+R is currently issuing construction document sets that are a hybrid of modelled systems with hand-drawn details, redefining the BIM implementation plan.

If the architecture profession embraces glass as a medium to facilitate the conversation between mind and hand, our craft has the potential not only to move into the territory of virtual space, but also to expand into modelling activities that forge new skills of sketching in 3D. It is only a small technological leap to imagine modelling digitally with a Pencil, but the impact this would have on our ability to critically think through space would be groundbreaking. When this is considered in combination with having the tools necessary to work in remote places, like the sketchbook, we might begin to question why architects as a profession are not leading the drive to develop better touchscreen technologies. In fact, with the tools available to us now, it is simply wrong that we use a mouse at all. ∆

It is only a matter of time before glass will move from a medium that we simply look through, to one that we actively work on; the architecture profession needs to recognise this opportunity.

Text © 2017 John Wiley & Sons Ltd. Images: pp 14-15 © Iwan Baan; pp 16-20 © Sean A Gallagher, Diller Scofidio + Renfro

**Péter Kis and
Sándor Bardóczi**

Geologic
Workfl

The Metamorphosis
of the Great Rock

Creating a series of inspirational museum spaces inside an irregularly shaped void at the heart of a massive artificial rock formation is no everyday task. To fulfil the dream that had driven construction of the Great Rock at Budapest Zoo & Botanical Garden over a century ago, and to make the most of the space available, local firm PLANT – Atelier Peter Kis devised an innovative workflow that began with 3D scanning of the decaying concrete structure. Architect **Péter Kis** and landscape architect **Sándor Bardóczi** describe it.

PLANT - Atelier Peter Kis,
The Great Rock,
Budapest Zoo & Botanical Garden,
Budapest,
Hungary,
2012

View of the main stairway from the lower level. The stair geometry is juxtaposed against the rock's interior structure and surrounding mesh.

Originally created during a major reconstruction of the Budapest Zoo & Botanical Garden between 1909 and 1912, the dolomite peak of the Great Rock was conceived in the shape of a limestone range. Covering an area of 4,700 square metres (50,590 square feet), with a peak height of 34 metres (112 feet), the plans were prepared more than 100 years ago by Gyula Végh, with zoological work supervised by Dr Adolf Lendl who was then director of the zoo.

During this three-year process, approximately 8,000 cubic metres (282,500 cubic feet) of concrete was poured. The rock crust itself was made from a 6- to 12-centimetre ($2^3/_8$- to $4^3/_4$-inch) thick Portland cement wire lattice structure by the same artisans who created the facade decorations of eclectic Budapest; with patterned rock cracks hiding the dilatation gaps of the structure. Unfortunately, Lendl's grand dream to construct a huge 30-metre (98-foot) long hall inside the hill in which to establish a Zoological Museum was suspended due to lack of money and the outbreak of the First World War. However, his ambition has now been fulfilled as part of the recent renovation of the Great Rock by PLANT – Atelier Peter Kis.

PLANT's design for the 'Magical Mountain' – a series of exhibition and assembly spaces within the synthetic geography of the rock – was created to allow for a unique and spectacular presentation of the special life forms that have inhabited our planet; where visitors to the zoo can engage 'wondrous rarities'[1] through the interactive exhibition system PLANT has designed within the space.

Design Process Then and Now

Not unlike the Renaissance artisans working on building problems before them, the design team at the turn of the 20th century relied on physical models to develop the structure. While drawings, now lost, were made, it was the models that conveyed their intentions to the artisans ultimately charged with constructing the rock, and which ensured a three-dimensional understanding of the scope of the work at a time when drawings did not figure prominently in the planning of buildings[2] – a process that can be seen as a metaphor for today's building information modelling (BIM).

above: The overlaid wireframe suggests the surprising presence of a cave hidden in the belly of the monolithic mass of the Great Rock – an adventurous construction from the heroic age of reinforced concrete originally completed in 1912. PLANT augmented this fascinating edifice with the practice's own ideas, contributing to the realisation of a 100-year-old dream: a Zoological Museum inside the extraordinary construction.

below: A three-dimensional survey determined the position of each node (x, y and z coordinates) via a point cloud which the design team utilised in the creation of a series of both digital and physical models, including at 1:100 scale to explore the relationship between structure and mesh.

In order for the reconstruction and renovation work to commence, a precise three-dimensional scan of the huge amorphous structure was undertaken by Dr András Tokody, a professor at Szent István University, in the late 1990s. His versatile surveyors – who were at once IT professionals, industrial alpinists and cave researchers – had to carry out their survey in below-zero temperatures within the belly of the concrete form. With his team, Tokody was able to develop a three-dimensional geometry-processing program showing the coordinates of the points defining the structure in a 3D point cloud, which at the time was considered quite innovative. They wrote a separate auxiliary program and built a geographic information system (GIS) database that assigned text-based metadata describing their condition and metric parameters to every structural component.

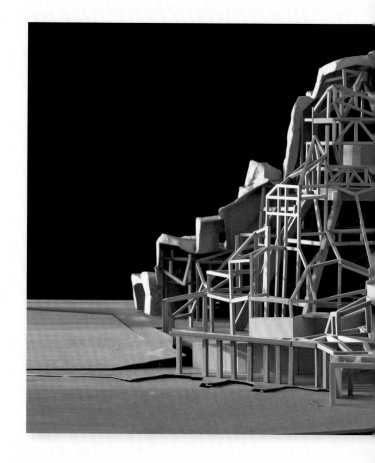

he three-dimensional
oint cloud was explored
n both 2D and 3D software
ackages to coordinate
tructural modifications to
he interior and visualise
he orientation of new
nterior spaces.

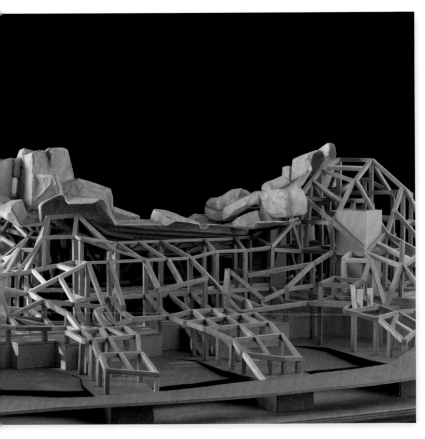

With the aid of the 3D point cloud, PLANT could determine the internal and external geometric volumes exactly, following the old structural framework. The 3D model and the plans, which were developed concurrently by PLANT, made it possible to keep the building's irregularly formed surfaces and structures under control, which was critical, especially during the construction phase.

The three-dimensional survey exposed a number of structural problems that PLANT needed to address to make the shell watertight again before design of the interior could begin. Utilising engineers with expertise in framework reconstruction, they opted to cover the net-like cracked external crust with a thin layer of sprayed mortar. Supporting beams were covered with a special plastic-concrete mix that stopped and even reversed the corrosion processes that had occurred over the last 100 years.

Design Workflow and Dramaturgy

PLANT's concept is a 'new' cave, carved into the volume of the rock to form a crystal-like structure that ties into the existing reinforced concrete. The shell of the new void is self-supporting, its structure following the reinforced framework of the rock's original organisation. The drawings produced are

right: The most unique moments within the restoration occur where the existing rock crust meets the supporting structural system and the new polygon mesh, which delineates the new interior spaces.

left: The main stairway, accessed from the entrance foyer, brings visitors up into the rock, where they experience the interior mesh that wraps the new programmatic spaces.

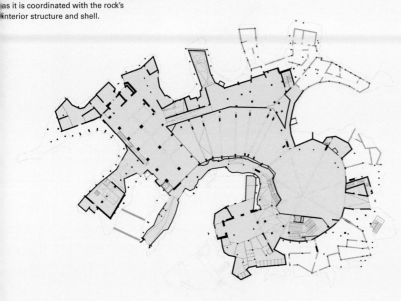

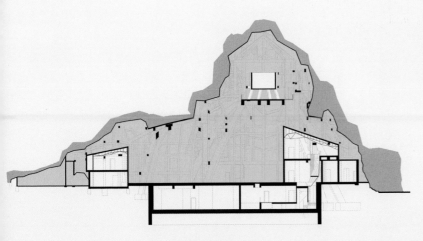

striking – merging almost geological principles with structural ones to propose a comprehensive building interior within the artificial hill, the programme for which began with the survey work and was finalised with the aid of non-standard design team members including a zoologist, geologist and games theorist.

The solid (rock) and void (cave) complement one another, their resolution going beyond the convention of one being positioned within the other. For the architects, dramaturgy had an important role to play, building on wandering and observation within the space to give the project the feel of a veiled object – one that is not fully understandable by being portioned within the interior. Visitors can continuously walk in and out of the new crystalline structure, providing the option to admire either the old or new structure, or both.

Following the completion of the design documentation, PLANT continued to be involved throughout the construction process, and the internal halls of the Great Rock were fully completed according to the final plans by 2012. The reconstruction added a further 3,200 square metres (34,400 square feet) of flexible internal space to the 1909 concept. The use of renewable energy also became a key aspect of the reorganisation. Heat from the thermal water feeding the Széchenyi Bath adjacent to the zoo, for example, has also been co-opted, with the inclusion of a heat exchange system, to supply conditioned air to the interior spaces.

Through the design and delivery workflow, the Budapest Zoo & Botanical Garden, which has continuously struggled with a lack of space, has gained several thousands of square metres of exhibition area, as well as the option for housing cultural and other educational events. The main structural elements supporting the Great Rock are highlighted throughout the reconstruction, and in the coordinated spaces an origami-like interior adds to the organically creasing boundary walls. The deep foundation of the framework made it possible to excavate a completely new level above the base structure, further increasing the already considerable internal volume. Light enters naturally from coordinated openings, creating a cohesive, exciting, playful, accessible and versatile string of spaces. Δ

Notes
1. www.zoobudapest.com/en/must-see/animal-kingdom/magical-hill.
2. Richard Garber, *BIM Design: Realising the Creative Potential of Building Information Modelling*, John Wiley & Sons (Chichester), 2014, p 32.

The

5

th

Stacie Wong

Engaging contractors early in a design process can resolve apparent mismatches between budget and programme and even enrich the design. But there are further benefits when this cooperation is followed through, with architects overseeing construction from a fully informed perspective – solving rather than creating problems for builders. **Stacie Wong**, a principal at New York design–build practice GLUCK+, explains.

Dimension
Architect-Led Design–Build

GLUCK+,
Dr Orrin H Pilkey Research Laboratory,
Duke University,
Pivers Island,
North Carolina,
2014

Addressing resiliency, structural integrity and durability were paramount for longevity in a hurricane-prone coastal environment with corrosive salt air and mould-inducing humidity. The building form is a metaphor for sea-level rise (SLR), in which the laboratory containing mission-critical equipment and irreplaceable specimens is elevated well above projected SLR and storm-surge levels, with the ground floor shaped to create outdoor porches protected from sun and wind.

Building information modelling (BIM) advocates the fourth dimension, time, to alleviate conflicts between the architect and contractor. While digital information exchange may lead to more coordinated buildings with fewer change orders during construction, which is important, it still does not tap into the full potential of true knowledge exchange between these two disciplines. Architect-led design–build (ALDB) posits a fifth dimension, one not readily detectable but equally powerful, in which the social capital and tacit knowledge of architect and contractor influence the built environment for the better.

ALDB places architects in the dual role of construction manager, responsible for design and documentation, and bidding and construction. ALDB is not a formula for elegant architecture or quality construction, though that can be the result. It is a mindset that can align aesthetic and technological conflicts within the logic of construction culture. When thinking and making do not readily match up, ALDB allows investigation, re-evaluation and project transformation in ways difficult to achieve when architects are relegated to a traditional role.

Closing the Gap

A gap exists between architects and contractors, though their work depends on each other. Architects' value is limited by separation from a body of information that can strengthen design and increase its relevance. Architectural thinker Thomas R Fisher asserts that design disciplines 'perpetuate an adolescent avant-garde that too often confuses the commission of errors with creative risk' and should instead 'take educated risks and eliminate avoidable errors, which demands ... work from knowledge rather than from the heroic lore that too often guides ... actions'.[1]

ALDB closes the gap using the social capital of architects and constructors working effectively together. In 1921, Austrian-British philosopher Ludwig Wittgenstein said, 'The limits of my language mean the limits of my world.'[2] Architects' capacity expands with proactive engagement with

GLUCK+,
Dr Orrin H Pilkey
Research Laboratory,
Duke University,
Pivers Island,
North Carolina,
2014

Every square foot mattered due to budget constraints, resulting in efficient and dual-purpose circulation with lab equipment maximised on wall surfaces, and mechanical, electrical and emergency power equipment protected indoors from salt air and hurricane damage. These constraints created design opportunities, allowing a level of abstraction with solid stacked boxes conveying SLR resilience, with entry demarcated as an open void at the heart of solid forms.

Duke University Marine
Laboratory Campus,
Pivers Island,
North Carolina,
2014

Situated on Pivers Island within the Outer Banks of North Carolina, Duke University Marine Laboratory Campus is a unique 'window on the sea', providing experiential learning that combines classroom with field and theory with practice, and encourages wise local land management and protection of natural resources due to engagement in the field. For the new research laboratory, every design decision reinforced the concept of providing a window on the sea, both figuratively and literally.

the messy world of construction. Subcontractors benefit from early participation, providing a forum for their technical input, for understanding project goals and their place in it. ALDB engages subcontractors early in the schematic design stage, incorporating their trade expertise to the mix. Their knowledge therefore shapes design rather than what is more typical, when they come in after the construction documents have been completed and begrudgingly find solutions to problems deeply embedded in the design.

In Evidence: Framing Problem and Solution

The Dr Orrin H Pilkey Research Laboratory, situated on Duke University's marine field campus on Pivers Island, North Carolina, is a case in point. It was completed in 2014 by GLUCK+ through ALDB, the final building solution emerging from direct engagement with the construction world.

Duke had mission-driven objectives: create a state-of-the-art laboratory enabling cutting-edge research; energise the campus and keep it competitive with a functional and programme-dense building; champion planning for sea-level rise (SLR); and demonstrate environmental responsibility through LEED Gold certification.

Duke also had programmatic and human-oriented goals: take advantage of the location's natural beauty; recognise that research is performed inside and outside the lab through debate and discussion; avoid an institutional feel; and embody the rustic sensibility of the original 1930s campus.

The location is demanding. Proximate to the Outer Banks barrier islands, environmental forces include hurricanes, high winds, corrosive salt air, withering sun and mould-inducing humidity. Situated in a small town, Duke wanted to utilise as many local subcontractors as possible despite the area's limited pool.

The building conceptually and programmatically addressed SLR by elevating the research laboratory to the first floor, thereby protecting expensive instruments and irreplaceable specimen collections well above 100-year flood and projected storm-surge levels. The ground floor was organised and specified to allow inundation without damage to service equipment or fixed building elements.

The building's solid expression was dual purpose – maximise wall space for equipment and storage while considering hurricane protection.

The ground floor is concentrated around social spaces. Coined by the then Marine Lab Director Cindy L Van Dover as the 'Collisional Commons', it is where ideas from the entire marine lab community collide informally. Visually and spatially porous, it opens to outdoor porches protected from seasonally shifting winds all times of day. The jagged footprint is better equipped than a flat facade to reduce storm-surge velocity. Surrounding landscape berms create higher ground to minimise scour along the building's edges, and the need for hard stormwater structures is removed through the promotion of infiltration at scupper discharge locations.

Meeting Duke's criteria, however, was not a linear path. The initial building concept looked very different than the end result due to ALDB.

Social Capital at Work

The dilemma: Duke's budget didn't match programmatic need. The objective: attract three new faculty members and their research teams. Designed on the heels of the 2008 economic downturn, the budget was fixed and extremely tight. The programme size was estimated to be

GLUCK+,
Dr Orrin H Pilkey
Research Laboratory,
Duke University,
Pivers Island,
North Carolina,
2014

The building envelope comprises only 17.5 per cent glazing to respond to programme, cost and resiliency demands, but glazing is strategically sized and placed for a spatially porous environment that opens up towards the water.

left: Developed on the heels of the 2008 economic crisis, the budget was fixed and modest, which made the architect-led design–build (ALDB) process critical to addressing budget and programme incompatibility. ALDB relies on access to subcontractors during the design period to obtain market feedback, and to allow early redesign without programme loss by reshaping the building and making the design better.

below: ALDB provides the design freedom to distil the building concept in direct response to market feedback from subcontractors.

37 per cent greater than could be afforded by the budget, loosely translating as the space for one new faculty member.

Rather than create a no-frills building to maximise the programme or one that embodied Duke's vision at the expense of a faculty member, ALDB challenged these assumptions. A larger building fulfilling the conceptual and aesthetic vision was designed, trusting that ALDB would tease out specific ways to attack the budget–programme misalignment. In other words, enter a pressure-cooker situation to extract the most important ingredients. And the pressure cooker was real, as it involved risk. The project had to be delivered with a guaranteed maximum price (GMP). If as architects GLUCK+ wanted to preserve the design and avoid the down-and-dirty, then as construction managers they had to figure out how to achieve it.

Steven Kotler, who focuses on the intersection of science and culture with emphasis on neuroscience and evolutionary theory, says that creative people problem solve by searching for 'dimmer connections, subtler relationships, novel linkages'. He says, 'When the brain encounters unfamiliar stimuli under uncertain conditions … baser instincts take over … [I]n an effort to save our own butts, the brain's pattern recognition system starts hunting through every possible database … Risk, therefore,

1

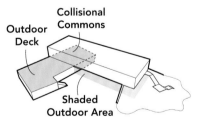

2

3

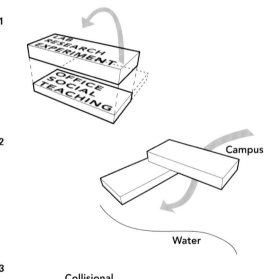

4

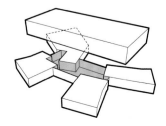

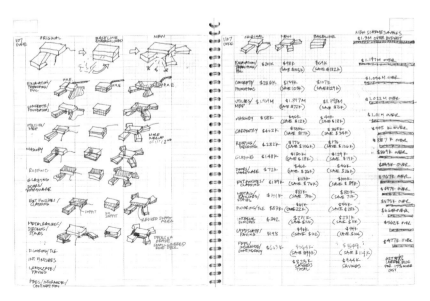

causes the mind to stretch ... think in unusual ways ... be more creative.'[3]

To discover what could be achieved in a small-town construction environment, a network of relationships with local subcontractors had to be established. The initial concept was documented via preliminary pricing sets identifying scope without getting bogged down in detail or coordination issues, and sent to local subcontractors. Once 'bids' were received, architects wearing the construction-manager hat sat with subcontractors identifying costs, trade by trade, and being open to comments and critiques of the design and suggested ways of reducing cost. The job then involved absorbing these different perspectives (understanding that something less expensive mechanically, for instance, isn't necessarily compatible with the less expensive carpentry solution), and making connections not readily apparent.

Pricing yielded a cost of $5.5 million – $800,000 over budget. Although the cost overrun was not as great as originally thought, cost reductions were imperative. A one-month redesign period ensued during which subcontractor comments shaped design thinking to make the building better, not just less expensive.

To reduce cost without programme loss, maximising the overlap of the ground and first floors was the most effective approach to shrink the building footprint, reduce the exterior wall area and decrease infrastructure runs. The ground floor was then reshaped to reintroduce spatial diversity. Through this back-and-forth process, the architecture team realised that the in-between spaces and not the overall building form were the essence of the design. This was only discovered through the ALDB pressure cooker. The building visually and conceptually became not only about

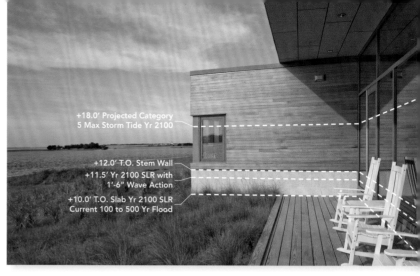

+18.0' Projected Category 5 Max Storm Tide Yr 2100

+12.0' T.O. Stem Wall
+11.5' Yr 2100 SLR with 1'-6" Wave Action
+10.0' T.O. Slab Yr 2100 SLR Current 100 to 500 Yr Flood

In addition to addressing the technical requirements for building in hurricane areas, 'soft infrastructure' solutions provided even greater resiliency. This translated to materials that can withstand flood water, and instead of presenting a flat, linear face to the water, the building's jagged edges can reduce the velocity of a storm surge, with landscaped berms creating higher ground to minimise scour along the building's edges.

below: The building structure and envelope address environmental forces, including hurricanes and wind. Analysis was complicated by decisions to 1) use wood-framed construction and concrete masonry foundations in response to dominant local construction techniques, 2) use 'stack boxes' that misaligned the ground-floor roof framing and first-floor slab framing on different elevational planes, and 3) introduce material transitions at critical heights as protection from potential water damage.

SLR, but about the collisional and collaborative nature of research. Construction knowledge, largely obtained via direct interaction with local subcontractors, honed the design.

Tacit Knowledge at Work

The process, however, was not completely reductive. While paring down yields more affordable design, the best solution is not always the least expensive. There are no explicit steps to determine what to remove versus maintain. It requires nuanced evaluation of how an architectural premise is reinforced by plan, section, construction detail, material selection, building technique, and the strengths and capabilities of local builders. In the case of the laboratory, this was necessary to contend with contradictory desires.

Faculty, for example, wanted storage and equipment. Large windows were viewed as wasted space. Major savings would undoubtedly result from reducing expensive hurricane-tested glazing systems. This, however, went against optimum natural daylight and views, and conflicted with the administration's desire to engage the coastal location. Ultimately, minimising glazing created simple, almost abstract forms, and windows were strategically placed for greatest spatial impact. When walking through the building, all comment on the feeling of openness without intuiting that glazing comprises only 17.5 per cent of the building envelope.

Addressing SLR on macro and micro levels is another example. The stacked box diagram achieved the macro, but the ground plane required the micro. Wave action was a concern even though well above the predicted 2100 sea level. The newly sculpted building shape reduces water velocity from shore, and surrounding dunes further dissipate forces. Zooming in, the ground floor visually and physically demarcates SLR datum outside and inside, protecting the building with a water-repelling concrete masonry unit (CMU) stem wall below datum, and moisture- and mould-resistant closed-cell spray insulation above.

This datum also addressed scale. The series of ground-floor boxes responds to the scale of other

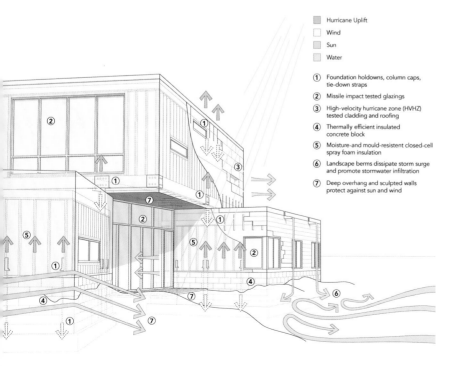

☐ Hurricane Uplift
☐ Wind
☐ Sun
☐ Water

① Foundation holdowns, column caps, tie-down straps
② Missile impact tested glazings
③ High-velocity hurricane zone (HVHZ) tested cladding and roofing
④ Thermally efficient insulated concrete block
⑤ Moisture-and mould-resistent closed-cell spray foam insulation
⑥ Landscape berms dissipate storm surge and promote stormwater infiltration
⑦ Deep overhang and sculpted walls protect against sun and wind

campus buildings, in spite of the project being the second largest on campus. The datum reduced the perceived vertical scale of walls, with the dunes further reducing scale, while doubling as effective stormwater management.

The above decisions met multiple criteria through the careful weighing of cost-effective and achievable ideas versus items impacting costs but imperative to design. Both the stacked box concept and material transitions are examples of this, being counter to hurricane resistance. The stacked boxes required double framing with lower box roof framing on a different plane to upper box floor framing. Material transitions created more situations requiring hurricane tie-downs.

Nicholas Carr, who examines technology's effect on cognition and capacity for concentration and contemplation, distinguishes between tacit and explicit knowledge. Tacit knowledge involves the things done without thinking such as eating and reading. These actions are learned, but once learned are automatically processed by the brain without conscious awareness. Carr says our ability to assess situations 'stems from the fuzzy realm of tacit knowledge. Most of our creative and artistic skills reside there too.'[4]

ALDB equips architects to evaluate and prioritise decisions. After years of experience in the office and field, designers adopting ALDB have variegated knowledge from which to distinguish big deals versus what can be accomplished with reasonable levels of detail and effort.

Hard Work and Feedback
Creative solutions require gaining knowledge, making connections and placing ourselves in pressure-cooker situations. But nothing replaces plain old hard work. Carr argues that 'immersive experiences … actively generate knowledge rather than passively take in information. Honing our skills, enlarging our understanding … require tight connections, physical and mental, between

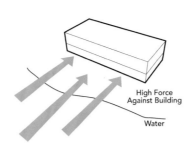

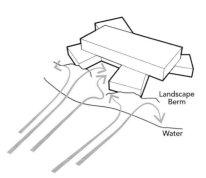

High Force Against Building

Water

Landscape Berm

Water

Stacked Blocks
High Velocity Unbroken

Sculpted Building
Velocity Dissipated

Taking a cue from buttress and channel systems found in coral reefs that reduce wave energies, the building form is sculpted to dissipate velocity and divert water that may surge inland during storms.

the individual and the world.'[5] Or, in the words of philosopher Robert Talisse, 'getting your hands dirty with the world and letting the world kick back in a certain way'.[6]

This leads to ALDB's ultimate power. It is not enough to access knowledge early on from subcontractors, but lack follow-through during construction. Social capital between architects and constructors exists only when working in two directions. Design is richer when informed by constructability. But the reality is that subcontractors, when faced with schedule pressures and field conflicts, will seek the easiest resolution possible, which isn't always best for the design, overall construction coordination or structural integrity of the building.

The architect being on-site, not as an observer but as an active participant in the supervisory role of construction manager, with full knowledge of the decision-making history and the overview on what needs to be achieved, is well-suited to resolving these conflicts. In this role, subcontractors view the architect as a problem solver, not problem creator.

With on-site responsibility for how something is built, information is collected that influences the next project. It is a knowledge-gaining feedback process that makes architects not only increasingly relevant, but increasingly creative. ⌂

Programmatic requirements were paramount with every design decision having to work within the limited budget. Faculty needed maximum real estate for equipment and storage, resulting in the strategic placement of windows at desk height to create unexpected framed 'windows to the sea' without sacrificing the programme.

Notes
1. Thomas R Fisher, *In the Scheme of Things: Alternative Thinking on the Practice of Architecture*, University of Minnesota Press (Minneapolis, MN), 2000, p 10.
2. Ludwig Wittgenstein, *Tractatus Logico-Philosophicus*, trans Charles K Ogden, Dover Publications (Mineola, NY), 1998, p 88.
3. Steven Kotler, 'Einstein at the Beach: The Hidden Relationship Between Risk and Creativity', Forbes, 11 October 2012: www.forbes.com/sites/stevenkotler/2012/10/11/einstein-at-the-beach-the-hidden-relationship-between-risk-and-creativity/2/#760ae6823c49.
4. Nicholas Carr, *The Glass Cage: Automation and Us*, WW Norton & Company (New York), 2014, pp 9–10.
5. *Ibid*, p 85.
6. Quoted in *Ibid*.

Adam Modesitt

Cenotaph for
Richard Feynman

Newark Bay

New Jersey

2016

A monument honouring the
life and work of the American
physicist Richard Feynman,
the Cenotaph is organised
as a system of distributed,
interconnected loadpaths,
a structural analogue to
Feynman's 'third way' path
integral formulation of
quantum mechanics. Sited
in the industrial context of
Newark Bay, it is composed of
over two million standardised
individual steel members that
aggregate into assemblies
and subassemblies of trusses,
each a unique configuration
consisting of thousands of
discrete components. The
project was enabled by a
custom workflow in Dassault
Systèmes' 3DEXPERIENCE
platform, developed to manage
assemblies of very large
numbers of components. All
project data and modelling
occurred in a cloud-hosted
database, without the use of
files.

Mashup and Assemblage in Digital Workflows

The Role of Integrated Software Platforms in the Production of Architecture

Digital technology is eliminating the separation between design and making that had existed since the Renaissance. But in order to seamlessly produce experience rather than just artefacts, architects have been turning to software developed for other fields. **Adam Modesitt** – assistant professor at the New Jersey Institute of Technology and founding principal of New York-based Modesitt Design – discusses the new directions that this hybridisation of workflows is allowing architecture to take.

To better understand the future of digital workflows in architecture, one place to start might be to look where they are altogether absent. Such practices are not easy to find. Digital workflows are so pervasive in architecture, engineering and construction (AEC) that examples of architects unaffected by them yet engaged in a contemporary discourse are rare. The Japanese architect Terunobu Fujimori stands out in this regard. With no office, and no staff, he operates in archaic fashion, rejecting most concerns of contemporary practice – modern materials, technologies, efficiency, scale, and even to a degree, usefulness. Known for teahouses and domestic-scale projects, his works conjure a nostalgic vernacular, but are in fact fanciful mashups of Western and Japanese histories, real and imagined.

His workflow appears to consist primarily of whimsical, freehand pencil sketches translated directly into built projects by his own hand, along with the help of an ad hoc menagerie of graduate students, local craftsmen, friends and neighbours, many of whom volunteer their time. Orthographic drawings of his projects surely exist, if unpublished, but one is left with the impression that most of the details are conceived of and built by hand onsite. A purist in the pursuit of this fanciful vernacular, he pleads with those who help him to construct his buildings 'to build, please, just a little more badly'.[1]

Fujimori divides all architecture into a binary of two schools of practice: the Red School, which he characterises as rugged, primitive, artless, natural and pulpy; and the White School, which is precise, smooth, sleek, innovative and modern.[2] But his embrace of the Red School is not just a rejection of Modernism; it is also a renunciation of an architectural workflow dating back to the 15th century, in which the architect and philosopher Leon Battista Alberti first advocated for the separation of authorship from making.[3]

Ultraviolet

In a much-discussed parallel, digital workflows also bypass Alberti's legacy. Through digital fabrication and construction, conceptualisation and implementation can become seamless, eliminating translative intermediaries like drawing sets. Digital workflows can re-engage craft, connecting design intelligence with material intelligence.

Terunobu Fujimori demonstrating the traditional process of making *shou sugi ban* (charred cedar planks)

Nagano

Japan

2015

Fujimori is the designer, craftsman and builder of his projects, experimenting with traditional methods and reworking them to create vernacular mashups.

Terunobu Fujimori

Yakisugi House
(Charcoal House)

Nagano

Japan

2007

The facade, floors and ceilings of the house are clad in Japanese chestnut, a wood rarely used in contemporary Japanese residential architecture, but common in the country's historical thatched-roof houses.

SHoP Architects

Software workflow
diagram

2012

A wide range of tools for
presentation, geometric
modelling, fabrication, file
management and 4D/5D
interweave and overlap. The
workflow is a custom mashup
of mostly familiar tools.

Digital workflows also allow architects to engage more than just craft, and to directly manipulate the vast flows of information of larger projects. Such projects require not only elaborate systems – egress, mechanical, electrical – but also involve scheduling, logistics, sequencing, cost, lifecycle and so on. Digital workflows can encompass all project-related information, including social interactions, at the earliest stages of design, integrating disciplines and expanding the territory of architectural production. As this engagement becomes increasingly seamless with conceptualisation, digital workflows begin to challenge the binary of Red and White, offering a foray into what we might call Ultraviolet.

How will architecture be impacted by widescale implementation of Ultraviolet workflows? A useful framework based on labour and production is proposed by Reinhold Martin.[4] Here, architectural production occurs on three interrelated levels: first, the production of objects (making); second, the production of signs (design); and third, the production of experience (affect). Since Alberti, architects have operated separately from the first level as 'immaterial labour', manipulating, communicating and processing abstract symbols to be eventually translated into manual, material labour on site. By operating in an archaic, pre-Albertian workflow, Fujimori's production of architecture acts on all three levels simultaneously as manual, 'material labour'. Digital workflows likewise allow architects to act on all three levels at the same time, but as immaterial labour, by utilising direct links between computers and making.

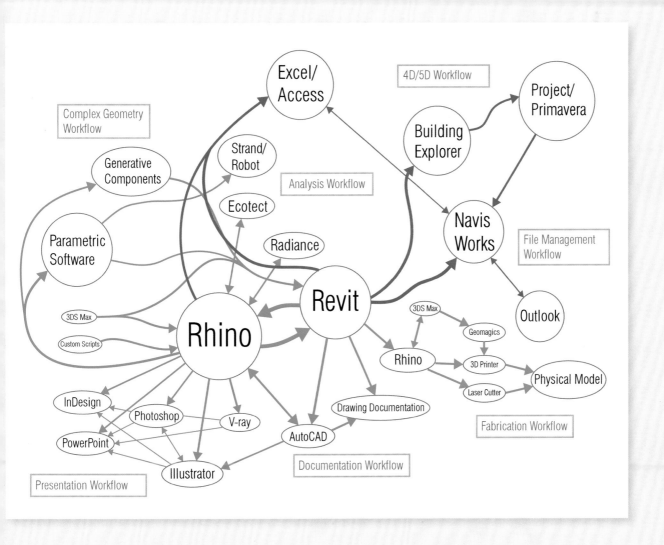

Adam Modesitt

Web interface

Dassault Systèmes
3DEXPERIENCE platform
project management
dashboard

Solar Decathlon
Studio

New Jersey Institute
of Technology (NJIT)

Newark

New Jersey

2016

Project management
dashboards aggregate data
on collective and individual
contributions to a project.
In addition to summary
analytics, digital models are
linked to scheduling tasks
and can be reviewed through
the web-based platform with
integrated messaging and
digital markup tools.

The development of software, the medium that synthesises immaterial design with immaterial making, offers further insight. Software made primarily for architects remains focused on design, and includes most building information modelling (BIM) software. It enables digital workflows, but otherwise maintains an Albertian mode of production, in which architects' immaterial design is translated to material labour at the level of making. Architects interested in more Ultraviolet workflows, however, have long looked instead towards software designed for and utilised in other fields, and especially the automotive and aerospace industries.[5]

The software of Dassault Systèmes is the most well-known example, famously first adopted by Frank Gehry in the early 1990s (and later distributed by Gehry Technologies, rebranded as Digital Project). Dassault Systèmes, along with PTC and Siemens, is one of the largest vendors of product lifecycle management (PLM) systems – the aerospace and automotive industry precursor and parallel to BIM. Founded to support the production of jet planes in the 1980s, Dassault Systèmes is at the time of writing larger in market capitalisation than Autodesk by 40 per cent.[6]

But Gehry's adoption of Dassault Systèmes' software was partial, as his practice maintained an Albertian model of production in which design intent was separate from making. Dassault Systèmes, like other PLM vendors, has for years advanced and developed a post-Albertian vision of digital workflow in which immaterial labour acts seamlessly across all levels of production. Moreover, it considers digital modelling and simulation ('digital mock-up' in industry parlance) to be solved problems, problems to look beyond. PLM industry leaders now emphasise instead the seamless production of affect. In this model, PLM goes beyond being only interoperable, disciplinary sets of tools tailored for the efficient production of artefacts. Instead, the digital production environment becomes a network for synthesising all forms of information across a single platform. Social, financial, distribution, branding and marketplace data are unified with the production process with the same level of integration as geometric and fabrication information. The platform is tailored to produce experience as much as it once was artefacts. Bernard Charlès, President and CEO of Dassault Systèmes, summarised this shift in a 2015 white paper: 'everything points to the current era as one of transition from a resource-based economy to an experience-based economy, in which the way we use and experience a product has more value than the product itself.'[7]

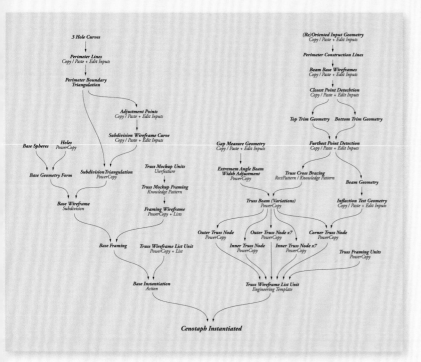

Workflow diagram labels

Left branch:
3 Hole Curves
Perimeter Lines
Copy / Paste + Edit Inputs
Perimeter Boundary Triangulation
Adjustment Points
Copy / Paste + Edit Inputs
Subdivision Wireframe Curve
Copy / Paste + Edit Inputs

Base Spheres
Holes
PowerCopy
Base Geometry Form
Subdivision Triangulation
PowerCopy
Base Wireframe
Subdivision
Base Framing
Base Instantiation
Action

Truss Mockup Units
Userfeature
Truss Mockup Framing
Knowledge Pattern
Framing Wireframe
PowerCopy + Lists
Truss Wireframe List Unit
PowerCopy + List

Right branch:
(Re)Oriented Input Geometry
Copy / Paste + Edit Inputs
Perimeter Construction Lines
Beam Base Wireframes
Copy / Paste + Edit Inputs
Closest Point Detechtion
Copy / Paste + Edit Inputs
Top Trim Geometry   Bottom Trim Geometry
Gap Measure Geometry
Copy / Paste + Edit Inputs
Furthest Point Detection
Copy / Paste + Edit Inputs
Extremen Angle Beam Width Adjustment
PowerCopy
Truss Cross Bracing
RectPattern / Knowledge Pattern
Beam Geometry
Inflection Test Geometry
Copy / Paste + Edit Inputs
Truss Beam (Variations)
PowerCopy
Outer Truss Node
PowerCopy
Outer Truss Node x7
PowerCopy
Corner Truss Node
PowerCopy
Inner Truss Node
PowerCopy
Inner Truss Node x7
PowerCopy
Truss Framing Units
PowerCopy
Truss Wireframe List Unit
Engineering Template

Cenotaph Instantiated

Adam Modesitt

Cenotaph workflow diagram

2016

Diagram of the relationship among templates in the Cenotaph workflow process. The Cenotaph was designed and constructed with multiple types of templates in the 3DEXPERIENCE platform, encapsulated through various methods (types listed below template names), and included design information such as subassembly geometry, wireframe structure, procedural logic and instantiation systems.

AEC as an industry is far less integrated than manufacturing, but as these tools are increasingly available to and adopted by architects, the emphasis on the production of experience raises questions for the direction of the discipline. What are the implications of tools that, rather than merely translating from design to making, seek to make seamless immaterial affective labour with immaterial making – that make immaterial material?

Immaterial Material

Since Alberti, drawing has been a primary means of exchange of information among the disciplines involved in the production of architecture, and correspondingly developed as the primary tool for conceptualising design; drawings both contain and generate design intelligence. As Ultraviolet workflows permeate the production process, they likewise increasingly become both a medium of production and a means for generating design intelligence. The generation of design intelligence emerges distributed from the medium, the structure of which formulates how architecture is both conceptualised and produced. As Ultraviolet workflows make production frictionless, the possibilities for architecture become untethered to traditional constraints such as trades and crafts, and practically unlimited. Instead, production becomes tied only to the forces of finance and marketplace. To adopt a platform that prioritises the seamless production of immaterial affect is to risk producing an architecture devoid of subject, or rather, that produces consumers as a subject.

Adam Modesitt

3DEXPERIENCE construction process geometry

Cenotaph subassembly

2016

Construction geometry consisting of points, lines and planes composes a network of parametric relationships to support subassemblies in the Dassault Systèmes' 3DEXPERIENCE platform.

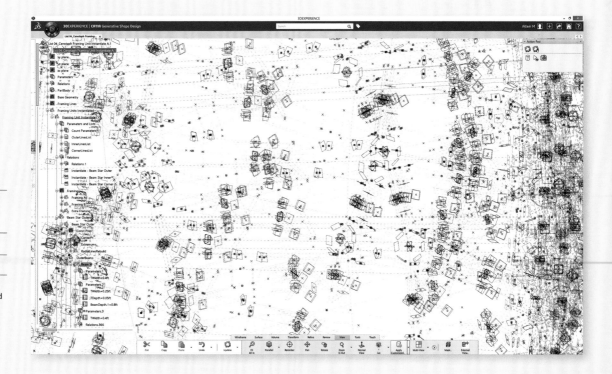

To adopt indiscriminate frictionless workflows tethered to market forces is to prioritise reproduction over production. Instead of the Modernist tradition of production for the masses, it is reproduction for the consumer. Martin characterises this effect as fetishisation of the supposed immateriality of immaterial labour, 'reproducing the world as it already exists: a world inhabited by consumer-subjects who imagine themselves as mass-customized "persons" on a parametric sliding scale, each thinking (or really, not thinking) a little differently.'[8] Indeed, this is essentially the vision of PLM vendors. No longer promoting tools that merely eliminate the friction between designing and making, they instead promote tools for the seamless production of consumer affect. Andreas Barth, Vice President and Managing Director of Dassault Systèmes, writes of the firm's new flagship platform 3DEXPERIENCE: 'the target is to provide the ability to place the customer at the heart of the system, integrating both company processes and product development processes … very good functionality is obviously not enough anymore'.[9]

The notion of consumers as subjects should give architects pause. How can architects develop new subjects within a platform that frictionlessly synthesises the production of consumer affect? Using platforms like 3DEXPERIENCE, other industries already seamlessly inform all levels of production with feedback loops of consumer affect, by farming consumer data, analysing online search behaviour, and quantifying interactions with 'deep-immersion' online virtual mock-ups. Moreover, platforms like 3DEXPERIENCE are drastically reducing the turnaround time between digital conceptualisation and high-realism, production-ready affective virtual realities. What are the implications if these workflows become the medium of architectural production, if data about 'magnetic' architecture is quantified, and new concepts can be measured against consumer metrics, the way cost and structure currently inform design?

Baja Bugs

Adoption of these platforms will not happen in AEC overnight, and these questions remain speculations about the future. Uptake will require a restructuring of supply chains, an overhaul of contractual arrangements, a transformation of design and construction practices, and perhaps even developments in artificial intelligence. But such speculation is important because an understanding of the medium can inform the process of adopting of new workflows.

below: The size and orientation of the holes in the perimeter of the Cenotaph are aligned to celestial objects referenced from Feyman's lecture series on classical mechanics. The composition of the truss-work between holes is driven parametrically by structural and fabrication constraints, which evolved in parallel with the design of the project. Small changes to the geometry of a single hole result in the reconfiguration of thousands of trusses, often in unpredictable ways.

bottom: View from the underside of the Cenotaph showing the structural transition from the spherical body to the three supporting vertical legs. The trusses transition in composition in response to structural load configurations, but remain composed of the same standardised members as the body of the Cenotaph.

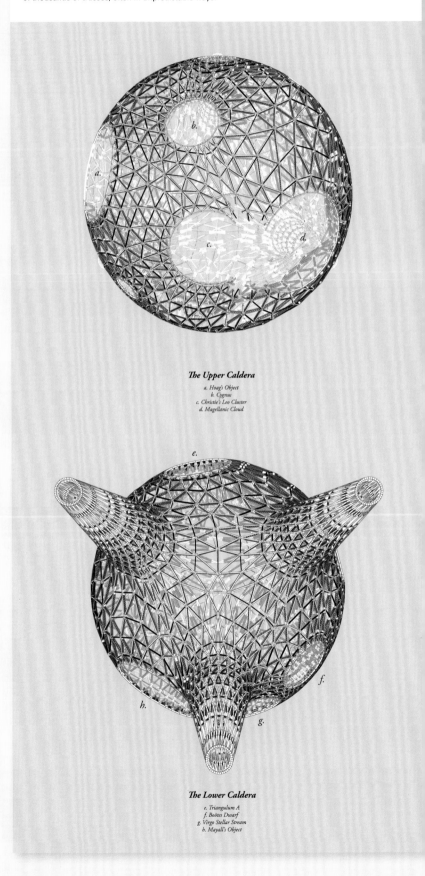

The Upper Caldera

a. Hoag's Object
b. Cygnus
c. Christie's Leo Cluster
d. Magellanic Cloud

The Lower Caldera

e. Triangulum A
f. Boötes Dwarf
g. Virgo Stellar Stream
h. Mayall's Object

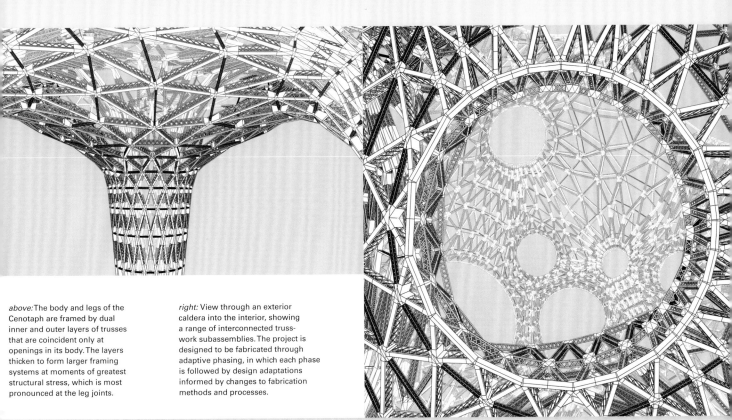

above: The body and legs of the Cenotaph are framed by dual inner and outer layers of trusses that are coincident only at openings in its body. The layers thicken to form larger framing systems at moments of greatest structural stress, which is most pronounced at the leg joints.

right: View through an exterior caldera into the interior, showing a range of interconnected truss-work subassemblies. The project is designed to be fabricated through adaptive phasing, in which each phase is followed by design adaptations informed by changes to fabrication methods and processes.

In the meantime, things are complicated. Architects at the vanguard of adopting aerospace production are nowhere near the integrated 'experience' workflows of other industries with highly integrated delivery chains. In reality, such workflows are a mashup of digital hybrids, cocktails of old and new methods. They also, by comparison, involve highly inefficient flows of information. Not cost inefficient, but the opposite. Architects run workflow chop-shops, taking latest tools and hacking them together on the cheap. Like the 'Baja Bugs' of the 1960s, they appropriate what they can afford and hack for performance, producing a blend of mass-produced parts, aftermarket parts and custom parts. At their best, they realign tradeoffs and break the rules, often to the point where the workflow is so hacked as to be only identifiable by the chassis.

These workflows reflect a friction of constraints among industry, design and expression, the trace of which is intrinsically manifest in the final building. They are scrappy, pushing tools to do what they should not, dalliances with different tools, non-committal to a single way of conceiving projects. Modelling in Maya, editing in Photoshop, diagramming in Illustrator, sequencing in GenerativeComponents, nesting in SigmaNEST, running routines in Excel, tweaking native NC code, then taking up with another toolset in the next project. Among architects there is hardly a single universalised workflow, and knowledge passes down primarily through people rather than encapsulation in software.

No single medium contains all information. The project exists piecemeal, in varied forms – in the parametric model, the initial diagram, the initial sketch rendering, the fabrication instructions, the wireframe model, the orthographic drawings. It exists in an assemblage of multiple, often contested images. These workflows intersect past and future, scripted and unscripted, experimental cocktails of information. The project contains a subject through the workflow. When computerised fuel injection became the norm in automobiles, hot rodding became a hybrid act of physical modding and computer hacking. Architects must likewise look for avenues to do the same, to introduce new friction within new workflows, to hybridise a system designed for seamlessness. Alternatively, we could always just take to heart Fujimori's advice and build, please, a little worse. ᗡ

Notes
1. Michael Buhrs and Hannes Rössler, *Terunobu Fujimori: Architect*, Hatje/Cantz (Ostfildern), 2012, p 56.
2. *Ibid*, p 54.
3. Richard Garber, 'Alberti's Paradigm', ᗡ *Closing the Gap*, March/April (no 2), 2009, pp 88–93.
4. Reinhold Martin, 'Postscript', in Peggy Deamer and Phillip Bernstein (eds), *Building (in) the Future: Recasting Labor in Architecture*, Yale School of Architecture (New Haven, CT), 2010, p 202.
5. Stephen Kieran and James Timberlake, *Refabricating Architecture: How Manufacturing Methodologies Are Poised to Transform Building Construction*, McGraw-Hill (New York), 2004.
6. Google Finance: www.google.com/: https://www.google.com/finance?q=OTCMKTS%3ADASTY&sq=Dassault%20Systemes.
7. Bernard Charlès, 'The Case For An Economy Driven By Innovation, Science, and Imagination', Dassault Systèmes, 2 December 2015, p 2: www.3ds.com/fileadmin/Stories/cop21/3DS-2015-BC-COP21-tribune.pdf.
8. Martin, *op cit*, p 204.
9. Andreas Barth, '3D Experiences: Dassault Systémes 3DS Strategy to Support New Processes in Product Development and Early Customer Involvement', in George L Kovacs and Detlef Kochan (eds), *Digital Product and Process Development Systems, Proceedings of the IFIP TC 5 International Conference, NEW PROLAMAT 2013, Dresden, Germany, October 10–11, 2013*, Springer (Berlin), p 24.

Putting BIM at the Heart of a Small Practice

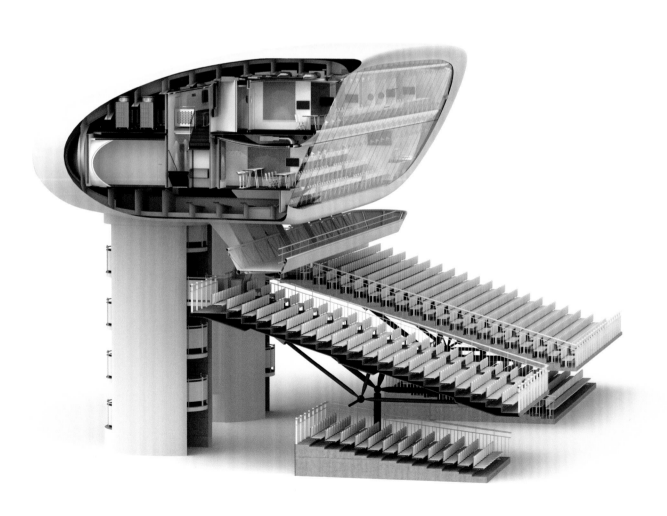

There can be advantages to being small. When the fledgling team of David Miller Architects in London realised that integrating building information modelling (BIM) into their workflow could enhance their efficiency and collaborative potential, they were able to bring about the changes much faster than their more established competitors might. Principal **David Miller** here describes the initiative – from an effective training schedule, to an interaction-inducing office environment, to a Best Practice Management System that helps keep up with RIBA protocols. Multiple repeat clients, and endorsements from external accreditation auditors, prove the effort was worth it.

At David Miller Architects, starting out as a small architecture practice in the mid-2000s, we realised that the commercial context in the UK presented some real challenges. We could see an increasing polarisation between small practices working on bespoke one-off projects while larger practices were sweeping up most of the available work through client framework agreements and partnering arrangements with large construction companies. Similarly, we could see a developing separation between the 'design' and 'delivery' functions of the architect, which seems to miss the point that both functions are interdependent and inform each other. It became clear that risk-averse procurement practices, especially on publicly funded projects, had the potential to constrain us or even lock us out. If we were to grow and get the opportunity to work on larger more interesting projects, we needed to find a way to disrupt the status quo. We believed that building information modelling (BIM) provided this possibility.

David Miller Architects

Refurbishment of the Media Centre

Lord's Cricket Ground

London

2017

Originally designed by Future Systems and winner of the Stirling Prize in 1999, this aluminium, 'semi-monocoque' building was groundbreaking, both in its design and in the boat-building technologies used. David Miller was project architect for the original building and in 2014 was asked to take on its refurbishment. Combining historical knowledge of the building with digital modelling and scanning techniques, it has been possible to increase the usable internal floor area by 15 per cent.

My own early career had been in the offices of Santiago Calatrava and Future Systems working on projects with complex geometry. So, from the inception of our practice we naturally used 3D tools to develop all of our projects. However, this was inefficient as we had to flip from one workflow to another to reverse engineer our 3D models into 2D drawings required by others. The tipping point with this approach was a pool house project for a private client. Originally a concept by Ushida Findlay Architects, the project was complex for its size, but we ultimately resolved it by bringing together a number of 3D digital models to address the coordination issues. This was when the penny dropped that as designers we can add considerable value through our ideas, but the time expended communicating these ideas erodes that value, and our fee. We needed to find a better, more streamlined way of working. The initial appeal therefore of what became BIM was the opportunity to work in a linear manner whereby the level of definition increased in a single environment without breaking the workflow. This included the opportunity to invite collaborators into that single environment.

As we searched for new techniques, it became apparent that change management was going to be our biggest challenge, as it is for any organisation when new ways of working are adopted. However, we also realised that as a smaller office we had an advantage; this was 2008 and as a team of just four people we were able to quickly make the decision to change, upskill the whole team in one go, then build on that as new people joined us. Speed and agility were luxuries that our larger competitors did not have.

Initiating Change

To initiate the change, we appointed a BIM champion to lead the process. She developed a bespoke six-day training schedule that was broken down into 40-minute modules, and she worked with the team on a one-to-one basis as and when a particular module was applicable to the task in hand. As the modules were short and relevant, they were always completed, enabling continuous improvement. Later she developed a three-day BIM 'boot camp' for new starters that involved full immersion before they had any project distractions. Once these skills were fully embedded in the office it was important for us to blow the BIM champion role apart and encourage different members of the team to lead on different parts of the workflow. That way we avoided introducing a BIM silo and it was possible for it to become 'business as usual'.

Obviously there has been an investment in tools and technology, but our experience is that at least half of our investment has been in training. This has been good for staff morale and wellbeing, and consequently for staff retention. Our team is relatively young so they have grown up with technology, which has also helped. It has been interesting to observe that as well as being permanently connected by it, they use technology to solve problems differently to people of my own generation. If they run into a problem their natural reaction is to try and go around it by looking for an alternative method. This digitally enabled inquisitiveness and very open peer-to-peer knowledge sharing leads to innovation. But the commercial environment within which we work can be fairly unforgiving, so it has been important for us to put a structured framework in place to allow innovation while staying commercially and technically on target.

In terms of virtual workflow, we reorganised all our processes around BIM. In the early stages of our adoption we developed an in-house BIM manual and BIM plan of work that defined inputs, processes and outputs for each RIBA work stage. These documents sat alongside our existing quality and environmental management systems and project checklists. However as the UK government's BIM Task Group began to define Level 2 BIM, we consolidated and merged all of our systems, checklists and trackers into a single Best Practice Management System (BPMS) with the Level 2 suite of documents at its heart. The resulting document is concise and in plain English, and contains embedded links to allow detailed review of the constituent documents. As a result of its accessibility, the BPMS ensures that all members of the team comply with protocols as a matter of course without requiring any specialist knowledge.

David Miller Architects
Anstey Hall Barns
Trumpington
Cambridge
England
2017

The team developed a collaborative, coordinated strategy to demonstrate that a fully digitised process is viable, achievable and beneficial on such a project, reducing waste, costs and time.

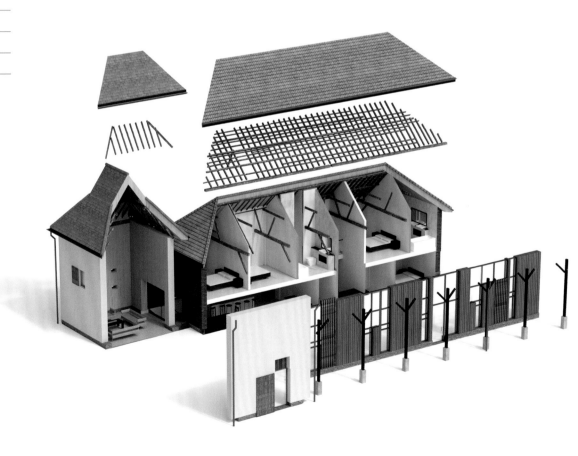

Additionally, we wanted to create an energetic environment that would help us attract and retain the best team. So we set about structuring the office around a customised BIM workflow both physically with our office set-up as well as virtually with the systems and processes we have put in place. We sought to create a collaborative and interactive 'mission room' space that encourages people to work together within our team and with our clients and co-consultants. We sit arranged around a single long table with a 30-metre (98-foot) magnetic white board running the length of the office interspersed with interactive projectors that give views into the computers. The intention is to get what is in the machines out into the shared environment. There are no walls or enclosed meeting spaces and all the business metrics are shared openly with the team, which helps break down hierarchies and encourages open and transparent working. This in turn feeds into a no-blame, incremental improvement culture that has been further inspired by Matthew Syed's book *Black Box Thinking* (2015).[1]

We have found that our approach has been very enthusiastically endorsed by the auditors for our external accreditations, ISO 9001, ISO14001 and, most gratifyingly, Investors In People who have upgraded us to Gold standard, which we understand to be very unusual for a smaller architectural practice. Indeed, external measurement and accreditation is important to us to drive continuous improvement, and in 2013 we undertook an audit by an external consultant to benchmark our BIM maturity. This used the US National Institute of Building Sciences – Facilities Information Council National BIM Standards (as UK standards were then still in development). At the time we achieved a Silver accreditation and put in place an action plan to achieve Gold. The evaluation allowed us to refine our workflow and team composition, target training and investment.

Has All This Effort Been Worth It?

In the earliest stages of BIM adoption we were able to reposition the practice by ensuring that our product – the information we produce – was more complete, coordinated and accurate. This was particularly important for us as a young practice if we were to be taken seriously. Then came the opportunity to offer additional and enhanced services, and this helped us to differentiate ourselves in the difficult trading

David Miller Architects office

Fitzrovia

London

below: The office is designed to encourage easy communication between the team. It is arranged around a single long table with a 30-metre (98-foot) magnetic white board running the length of the office interspersed with interactive projectors that give views into the computers. The intention is to get what is in the machine out into the room.

right: The team have grown up with technology as well as being permanently connected by it. Their approach is to work around a problem by looking for alternative methods. This technology-enabled inquisitiveness and open peer-to-peer knowledge sharing leads to innovation.

environment post-2008. Further along in our adoption journey, in 2011 when the UK government announced that it would require Level 2 BIM on all publicly funded projects from April 2016 onwards, we targeted and achieved early compliance, giving us a further competitive edge.

By reviewing metrics from our audited accounts, business improvements have included higher levels of efficiency demonstrated by a year-on-year increase in turnover of around 20 per cent, and higher-value, more complex projects being won and delivered. Some of this may be a consequence of a small firm growing, but that is arguably a consequence of adopting these new processes. The most important metric is that over 80 per cent of our business comes from repeat clients, demonstrating high customer satisfaction levels. We have been very open in sharing this information, because we believe it shows the business case for BIM adoption and has the potential to bring more collaborators and clients into the space.

Interrogating the numbers in more detail, we see that we have consistently spent £30,000 per annum since 2008, with 50 per cent of that investment in training; the software and hardware costs are fairly manageable. At the beginning this was 12 per cent of our turnover; it is now 2 per cent, so the pain does go away. Similarly, reviewing fee income against BIM costs we see that

The most important metric is that over 80 per cent of our business comes from repeat clients, demonstrating high customer satisfaction levels.

David Miller Architects	Cambridge
Anstey Hall Barns	England
Trumpington	2017

The conservation and refurbishment of a group of historic barns and other agricultural buildings dating from the 18th century provide eight luxury conversions, with a further four new homes on the site.

in the early stages while we were learning, costs and income stayed parallel; however, once we were more experienced we started to see real efficiencies. During the adoption period we have carried out a lot of R&D, we have gone forwards, gone backwards and certainly made some mistakes. Consequently we probably understand our business much better. However, we wish we had started out with the guidance and clarity on BIM adoption that is now available – with a little effort it would be possible to collapse our years of work into weeks.

We have learned that it is possible to create a robust, companywide blueprint for a smaller practice that integrates BIM into the workflow and creates a new and better 'normal' way of working. The BIM-centric enterprise model holistically encompasses our methods, our team, our working environment and our external interfaces. This has promoted stronger collaboration with our clients and consultant partners and allowed us to offer them new services that add value and reduce risk. These outcomes, backed up by metrics, also demonstrate that the UK government's BIM targets for 2016 are achievable and make economic sense, and clear leadership from government has empowered us. This also shows that small and medium-sized enterprises can take the lead on industry-wide programmes and innovation through adopting a digital approach; organisation size is not a barrier.

A Sustainable Small Practice

It would be fair to say that we have been driven by the commercial imperative to develop a sustainable business model for our emerging practice to achieve future growth aspirations.

However, from the start we wanted to seize the opportunity that this climate of change presented to establish a new, more satisfying way of working as architects, opening up new career paths for young professionals, creating new business opportunities and working in an industry that would be more collaborative and less adversarial. A BIM workflow has been the enabler. ⌂

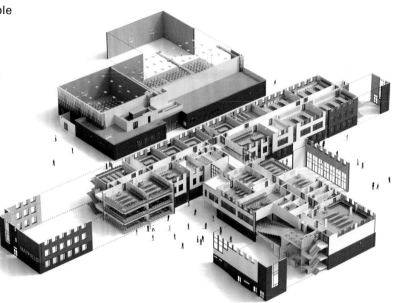

David Miller Architects
Mayfield School
Redbridge
London
2014

right: Mayfield meets the school's educational needs as well as their ambition to create a 'culture of aspiration'. It provides uplifting and flexible teaching spaces and a new social 'heart' arranged around a Hellerup stair.

below: With just 17 months available for design and delivery, and a very tight budget, a standardised solution seemed the only option for the Mayfield School project. However, by embracing digital design and off-site construction from the outset, it was possible to provide a bespoke design and urgently needed school places in one of London's most under-pressure boroughs.

Note
1. Matthew Syed, *Black Box Thinking*, John Murray (London), 2015.

3NCRYPT3D

WORKFLOW5

The Secret World of Objects

Specific Objects is a New York-based interdisciplinary design practice. **Rhett Russo**, one of its directors, is developing architectural assemblies that are informed by the specific properties of ceramics, how these traits become encrypted through technology, and at what cost. Drawing on the philosophical writings of Tristan Garcia, Bernard Stiegler and Graham Harman, the art of Jiří Kolář, and a competition design by his own firm, he explores ways that the peculiar nature of objects initiate new workflows.

Jiří Kolář

Hand

1969

The 'rollage' techniques Kolář developed to combine images are the product of a simple mathematical method that employs multiple copies. The sequencing of the copies is often intentionally altered to further emphasise the strange aesthetic features of the images themselves.

In his book *Form and Object* (2014), the French philosopher and novelist Tristan Garcia describes two realms of being, one in which objects are unequal and irreducible, which he associates with 'chance', and the other realm in which forms are equal and flat with a 'price to pay'.[1] Garcia's surprising assessment of the flat world includes form and by extension all of its protocols that serve to codify and reduce objects to their relations. By offering chance, objects like architecture come with an inherent price to pay; a need for certainty and the reduction of things to forms. From this perspective, workflows are formations, which tend to render things flat and rob them of their surprise.

Garcia makes a related claim that the value of things is not given to things by non-things, 'subjects, consciousness, interests, structures, or models of equilibrium, but that their value is *situated in the things themselves*'.[2] The potential has always existed for the chance of things to be transferred to the realm of architecture. This alternative requires a process of encryption that engenders objects rather than encasing them in certainty. This should not be misunderstood as an abandonment of economy, but rather an opportunity to construct an alternative economy from objects themselves that is undetectable to thoughts and words.

For any object whatsoever, chance is a state of being and it plays a key role in shaping the evolution of modernisation and protocols of control. Consider the invention of the Bézier curve, which the mathematician and engineer Pierre Bézier introduced while working for Renault during the 1960s.[3] These non-rational curves came to certify the aesthetic of the Renault automobile. By minimising chance, his regime became a means for specifying consistent curvatures in metal. Bézier's innovation is not without a price to pay. His algorithm replaced an individualised history of designing and manufacturing objects manually. Bézier's chance encounter with the aesthetics of the automobile led to a relatively small amendment to a workflow that eventually became a formula for drawing curves everywhere.

There are at least two significant shortcomings of workflows. The first concerns the presence of flat ontologies, where mass-produced objects appear anywhere and everywhere in the form of undifferentiated responses to specific problems. Chance encounters are frequent, intentionality is undetectable, and risk and reward are low. In this scenario, the means of specifying resemblance take precedence over the objects being specified. The second scenario is characterised by what the philosopher Bernard Stiegler refers to as the entropy of algorithmic processes – such as Google Translate, in which English is a pivot language for translation – where there is 'a submission to the law of averages'.[4] Here, the shotgun promise of more options is coupled with the flexibility to

It is not uncommon for good design to be equated with a workflow that consists of a measurable or repeatable set of routines. The principle that a workflow can somehow produce good architecture, however, is an unnecessary burden. Architecture, like any other object, cannot be reduced to its relations. If we continue to correlate the value of an architectural object with its protocols and organisational processes, it will not be without a price to pay. The architecture profession has started to return to workflows that are specific to the realm of objects and the chances they withhold. These terms, once the enemy of technical routines, will no longer remain allusive to the next generation of machines. Insofar as set procedures continue to be replaced by innovations, they are no less durable or meaningful than the art and design processes that employ them. By taking the chances in things and fusing them into new objects, architects develop forms of objectivity in the aesthetic realm, outside of reason or protocols of production. This alternative form of workflow is not geared to solving problems. While it is specific, it is also encrypted, vicarious and unrepeatable.

accommodate chance encounters with any economic, political or material instability, which might delay the delivery of any entity – including architecture. Intentionality may initialise a workflow, but it struggles to manage its aesthetic qualities. The price to pay is that these workflows are intensive, they often cannot be reused, and much time is spent insulating their parts from extensive encounters in order to stay ahead of the system.

TH3 FUTUR3 OF TH3 OBJ3CT

An altogether different approach towards the flatness of things can be found in the art of Jiří Kolář. The Czech poet and master of collage was visionary in his combination of images, objects and written words, and well known to a generation of architects. Among the most notable forms of collage he invented are rollage, chiamage and crumplage, 'that have assumed the attributes of things'.[5] Rollage is often developed by slicing up a masterwork, such as a Botticelli, Leonardo or Poussin, and recomposing it using multiple copies. Parts that are not adjacent in the original composition bear a new and often strange symmetrical and serial relationship to other parts. 'The illusionist picture space of the original is converted into an abstract flat and artificial space. Rhythm, movement and vibration enter into the picture simultaneously, thereby revealing it in a novel, dynamic form.'[6]

Kolář's development of rollage was a significant departure from the collage techniques of the Surrealists and Dadaists: 'the materials employed by Kolář never try to look like anything but what they really are – the materials themselves and never the images they evoke'.[7] The poetry of rollage rests in its presentation of the copy as a thing in itself. Regardless of whether the image is presented in part or whole, all copies are granted the same status. By mechanically assembling the fragments of images, Kolář was able to restore the objects' ability to communicate, something that he achieved in part by minimising his role as an author and artist and placing emphasis on re-presenting past works. In short, rollage is a form of encrypted object that allows one compact copy to vicariously amplify its aesthetic potential multiple times – once in the form of the copies and once more as an unforeseen and carefully choreographed image.

MAT3R1AL OBJ3CT5

A key observation in the work of philosopher Graham Harman's development of speculative realism is that the only contact we have with objects is indirect, and he extends indirect causation to include interactions between non-human entities as well. According to Harman, real objects cannot be fully known; whether real or virtual, they exist independently outside our mind and insofar as objects withdraw from consciousness, they can surprise us.[8] This is a key aspect of any design process that prioritises the interactions of real objects over thought. Encrypted workflows that are associated with material practice share several characteristics. First, they are formulated through a direct knowledge of how things interact. Second, they are predicated on a language of repeatability, but more often resemble recipes that accept variation. And third, they tend to resist abstraction. Encrypted workflows are designed to address the strange particularity of any object and its specific interactions with other objects.

Encryption is no stranger to architecture. One of the earliest examples of encryption dates from 1500 BC, and it includes a camouflaged recipe for a secret pottery glaze, in full view on a wall in Mesopotamia.[9] Because of the overall unpredictability of materials such as ceramic or cement, material workflows evolved through experimentation and the search for secret recipes that could not be reproduced. Herein is one of the key distinctions between the praxis of art and architecture: for a ceramicist, the realm of possibility belongs to vibrant matter that is inherently hidden and anexact; that is, essentially rather than accidentally inexact. Conversely, architectural production resides in exactness and the realm of fixed specifications. There are many practical reasons for this but, independent of any praxis, the aesthetic possibilities of objects belong to a surplus of possibility that is equally flat and independent from our own judgement. In order for our discipline to evolve, we need to embrace the idea that there are simply no flaws in things, only chances.

Specific Objects

Museum of Underwater Antiquities Competition

Piraeus

Greece

2012

The competition brief for this proposal called for the adaptive reuse and urban renewal of the port of Piraeus. Visible from offshore, the museum was conceived as an addition to an existing 26-metre (85-feet) deep concrete cereal silo for the exhibition of objects lost at sea.

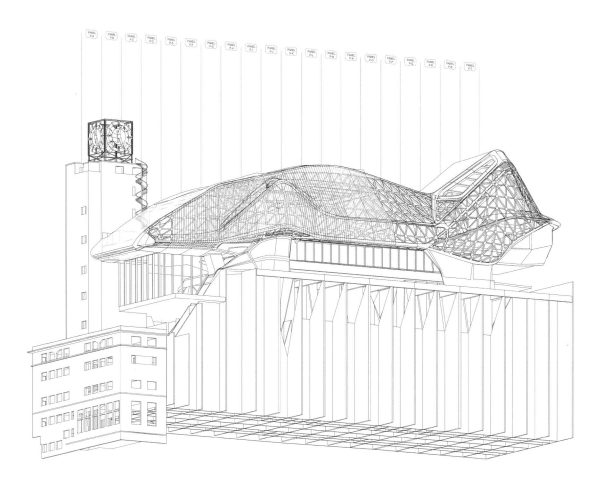

The panels in the diagram are labeled: PANEL P-A, PANEL P-B, PANEL P-C, PANEL P-D, PANEL P-E, PANEL P-F, PANEL P-G, PANEL P-H, PANEL P-I, PANEL P-J, PANEL P-K, PANEL P-L, PANEL P-M, PANEL P-N, PANEL P-O, PANEL P-P, PANEL P-Q, PANEL P-R, PANEL P-S, PANEL P-T

COP135 OF COP135 B3COM1NG OBJ3CT5

The workflow that was originally developed by the interdisciplinary design practice Specific Objects in their competition proposal for the Museum of Underwater Antiquities in Piraeus on the outskirts of Athens (2012), allows a closer look at how the specific features of objects become encrypted. There are two things to note about the building. Foremost, the museum's primary mission was to conserve and exhibit artefacts that had been lost at sea and, second, the building is located within the abandoned concrete silos of an existing cereal factory. Oddly, the proposal involved the transformation of a place once used to house agricultural surplus to a place for curating maritime artefacts. Most importantly, it is through the vicarious and accidental fate of the pottery, vessels and weapons lost at sea that these fragments became found objects for speculation.

The encryption is concerned with the objectivity of the building's ceramic envelope and the aesthetic genre of underwater artefacts. As a family of fragments, these objects have a unique patina, size and texture that became central to the design of the envelope. The building's shell is conceived as a

hybrid of two plastic materials: lightweight precast concrete panels on a 4-metre (13-foot) module and an embedded layer of multi-coloured, press-moulded ceramic tiles approximately 30 centimetres (12 inches) wide. The process of embedding large panels of glistening blue ceramic within an uneven stucco wall was developed in Samarkand during the 14th century.[10] The design of each of the museum's tiles is unique in its profile, depth and colour. To achieve this, Kolář's rollage technique was adapted to slice multiple copies of a thin slab of press-moulded clay. Under normal circumstances this degree of variation would be prohibitive; however, in this case it is possible to construct a single large ceramic 'mother-mould' and to press-mould multiple copies that are further multiplied by numerically slicing the clay at intervals such that no tiles are the same. Through an aesthetic engagement with the object, a new economy was developed.

The plastic nature of the clay enables it to be post-formed, or draped, to meet the precast panels. It is in the presence of the architecture that these features are brought into brief contact with the plastic agencies of the concrete, the encrusted qualities of the press-moulded ceramic, the aesthetic economy

A customised workflow was developed to divide the envelope into individual panels. The building envelope comprises 4-metre (13-foot) wide, precast concrete panels surfaced with press-moulded ceramic tiles. Each tile is cut from a single press-mould and finished with different glazes.

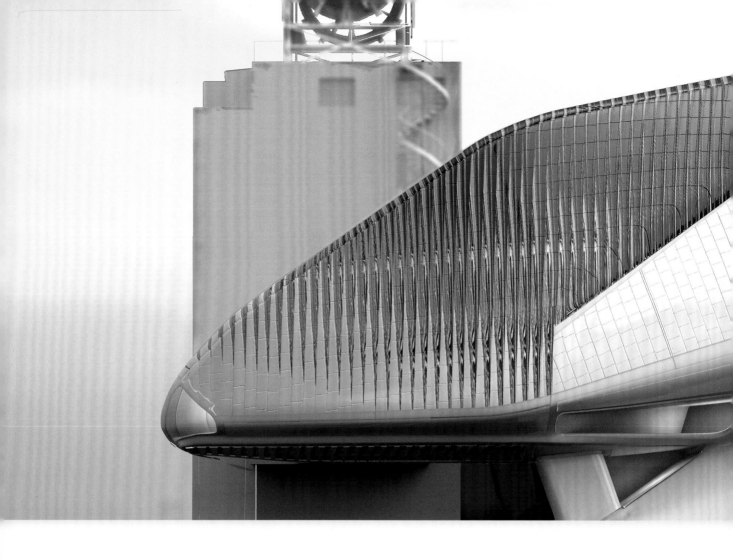

Specific Objects

European Ceramic Workcentre

Oisterwijk

Netherlands

2016

above: Inspired by the strange relief of the underwater artefacts, the ceramic tiles in this proposal are designed to encrust the surface with reflections, and to provide a modulated relief that contrasts with the diffuse surface of the precast panels.

right: The 82-metre (270-foot) long, west facade seen from the northwest. A shimmering reflection is achieved by combining the diffusivity of the precast surface with the modulated colours of the three principal ceramic glazes.

TH3 3NCRYPT10N
15 CONC3RN3D
W1TH TH3
0BJ3CT1V1TY OF
TH3 BU1LD1NG'5
C3RAM1C
3NV3L0P3 AND
TH3 A3STH3T1C
G3NR3 OF
UND3RWAT3R
ART3FACTS.

Specific Objects

European Ceramic Workcentre

Oisterwijk

Netherlands

2016

Unique tiles are cut from a single press-moulded
ceramic 'mother-mould'. After the clay reaches a
stable state, it is numerically sliced to produce copies
that each contain unique relief work. Nine copies are
pressed from the single 'mother-mould'. To achieve
subtle changes in the relief, the moulds are offset
and sliced into 30-centimetre (12-inch) strips that are
then interleaved to yield 245 unique vertical strips.

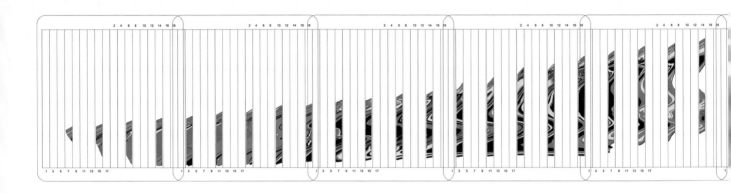

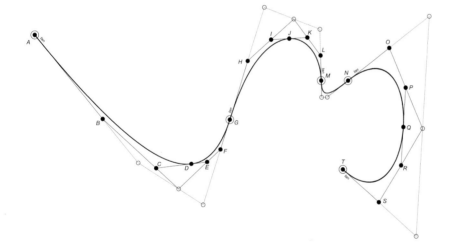

Specific Objects

Diagram of a complex Bézier curve

2016

left: Pierre Bézier's algorithm for constructing
a curve uses tangents that can be interactively
repositioned through the use of control points.
Prior to Bézier's invention, analogue versions
were constructed using metal and wood to
construct complex curvatures manually. In
contrast to the precision of the Bézier curve, the
workflow associated with the tiles for Specific
Objects' proposal for the European Ceramic
Workcentre utilises the anexactness of the clay
to develop new assembly methods.

Specific Objects

European Ceramic Workcentre

Oisterwijk

Netherlands

2016

right: Image indicating where the
glazes are added after the tiles are
cut. The CNC (computer numerical
control) positive forms the basis
for the negative rubber mould. The
interspersed character of the glazing
allows for colours to be precisely
intermixed across the entire facade.

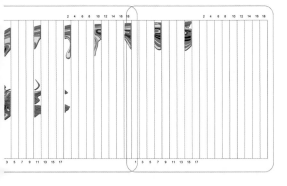

of the rollage and the fragments that constitute the collection. At this juncture, it is worth asking how any part of this chance encounter between the features of the sea and its materiality is brought to bear on the workflow. The simple answer is that any speculation of this sort is only possible when there is an infinite number of chances, an embrace of the material's agency and no formal workflow for bringing them together.

ARCH1T3CTUR3 1N 5URPLU5

Architecture no longer represents a singular ideal, and as such it should separate itself from the certainty we expect from workflows. Being equipped with a sense of what any material might do or become, comes with an opportunity to speculate on new ways for the basic features of a ceramic object, or any other form of matter, to come into contact with other objects and their assemblages. It is through this surplus of actions and agencies that one can begin to formulate and encrypt alternative forms of knowledge within the container that is recognised as architecture. The facts that threaten the integrity of any object are the same facts that can be instrumentalised to exceed our expectations. As Garcia points out, this objectivity occurs through the transformation of things to objects, and it is not without a price to pay. ᴓ

Notes
1. Tristan Garcia, *Form and Object: A Treatise on Things*, trans Mark Allan Ohn and Jon Cogburn, Edinburgh University Press (Edinburgh), 2014. See also Graham Harman, 'Object-Oriented France: The Philosophy of Tristan Garcia', *Continent*, 2 (1), 2012, p 8. Features of Garcia's ontology concerning 'chance' and 'price to pay' were brought to my attention by Harman.
2. From Garcia, *op cit*, p 334.
3. Gerald Farin, Josef Hoschek and Myung-Soo Kim, *Handbook of Computer Aided Geometric Design*, Elsevier Science (Amsterdam), 2002, p 4.
4. Sam Kinsley, 'Bernard Stiegler: "The Time Saved Through Automation Must be Granted to the People" [translation]', 18 July 2016: www.samkinsley.com/2016/07/18.
5. Weiland Schmied, 'Introductory Collage', *Jiří Kolář*, The Solomon R Guggenheim Museum Foundation (New York), 1975, p 13.
6. *Ibid*, p 14.
7. *Ibid*, p 13.
8. Graham Harman, 'On Vicarious Causation', *Collapse*, 2, 2007, pp 171–205.
9. Gerhard Strasser, interviewed in Kaveh Waddell, 'The Long and Winding History of Encryption', *Atlantic*, 13 January 2016: www.theatlantic.com/technology/archive/2016/01/the-long-and-winding-history-of-encryption/423726/.
10. Anne Berendsen, *Tiles: A General History*, Viking Press (New York), 1967, p 24.

above: A single strip of tiles showing the reveals and separations between glaze colours. A workflow was developed to maximise the number of unique tiles from one mould through the use of wire cutting. Individual tiles can be pressed flat, face down into the mould. Later in the drying process, they are placed face up on a mandrel to marry the curvature of the underlying panel geometry. The plasticity of the clay allows for any element to be uniquely bent or 'draped', thus avoiding a need for channelling the substrate.

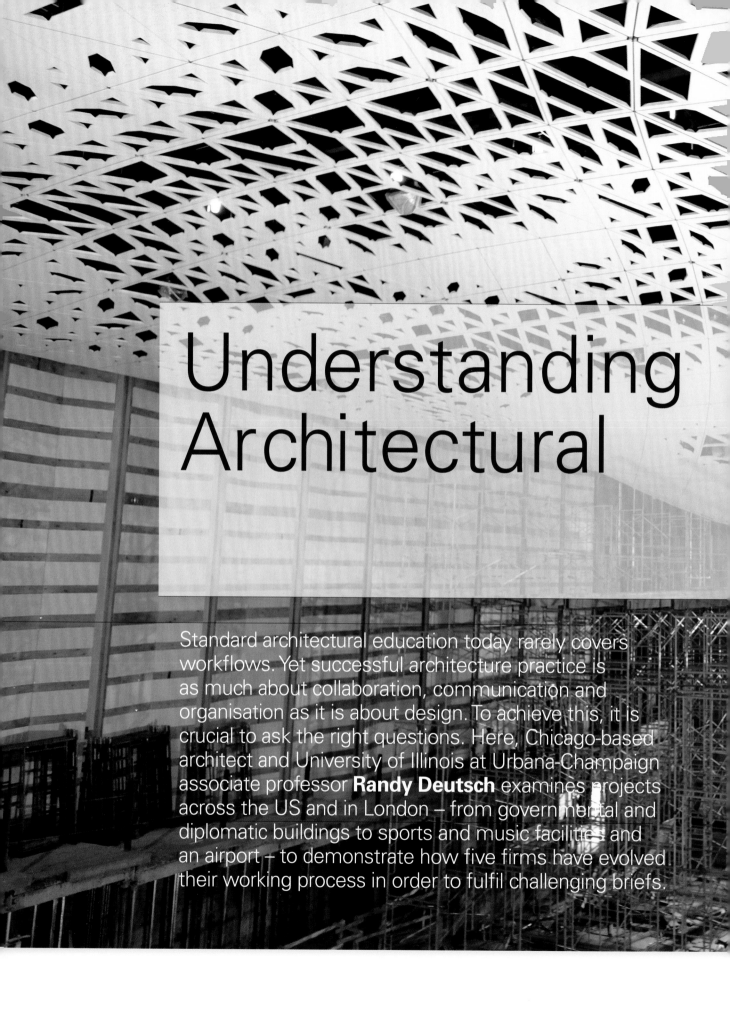

Understanding
Architectural

Standard architectural education today rarely covers
workflows. Yet successful architecture practice is
as much about collaboration, communication and
organisation as it is about design. To achieve this, it is
crucial to ask the right questions. Here, Chicago-based
architect and University of Illinois at Urbana-Champaign
associate professor **Randy Deutsch** examines projects
across the US and in London – from governmental and
diplomatic buildings to sports and music facilities and
an airport – to demonstrate how five firms have evolved
their working process in order to fulfil challenging briefs.

Randy Deutsch

Workflows in
Global Practice

Krueck + Sexton Architects,
Benjamin P Grogan and Jerry
L Dove Federal Building,
Miramar,
Florida,
2015

below and opposite: Three distinct conceptual designs – high, medium and low, all based on a narrow office wing typology – were developed for architectural peer review during concept design.

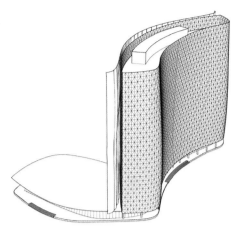

Practising architecture today requires an equal emphasis on both product and process, where architectural inquiries need to answer not only what, but, importantly, how. How did this particular building or building component come about? How did the forces that come together at the start of any project arrive at that outcome? How did the firm get things done? Due to the advent of digital technologies and collaborative work processes, it may sometimes seem like the emphasis is on process over product: or even further yet, where process is the new product.

The question 'how' is one about workflows. In particular, new workflows brought about not only by the emergence of building information modeling (BIM) and computational design, but by the convergence of multivariate technologies and work processes.

Architecture schools tend to address topics separately, by the professor's speciality, the dictates of the curriculum, university or accreditation board. Once students have had a chance to work in an architecture or engineering office – over the summer or between school years – they discover that what is not offered in school is learning how to work with others on collaborative teams; how files are shared; BIM etiquette; and how projects are

organised for greatest efficiency and effectiveness. In other words – workflows. Recent graduates identify understanding workflows as the subject they wished they had known more about in school so that they would be better prepared for working with others in a practice setting.

Understanding these shifting workflows does not guarantee that architects will gain ground and reap the rewards, but instead provides a window, opening or opportunity that they can either rise to – or let pass. The projects below highlight how five firms have succeeded in navigating and mapping emergent workflows. As Guest-Editor Richard Garber states in the Introduction to this issue of *D*: 'Workflows, in fact, are a kind of hidden phenomenon in completed buildings. Buildings alone, especially complex ones, cannot convey the collaborative activities that design teams have developed in the service of construction execution' (p 10). To this end, this article attempts to accomplish two things: to expose the work processes that until now had been hidden in the built form; and to provide a series of questions that architects – and architects-in-the-making – can use both to understand their own workflows, and to describe, explain and justify their workflows to others.

Exterior fixed sunshades, made of perforated aluminium, reduce heat load and glare inside.

Practising architecture today requires an equal emphasis on both product and process, where architectural inquiries need to answer not only what, but, importantly, how.

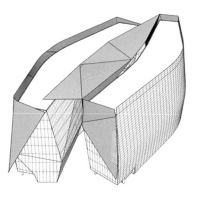

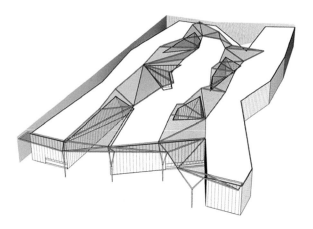

Beyond Technical Workflows: The Strategic and Tactical

Krueck + Sexton Architects' design for the Benjamin P Grogan and Jerry L Dove Federal Building in Miramar, Florida (2015) was driven by a desire to represent the dignity, vigour, enterprise and stability of the US Government. They focused on maximising daylight, minimising energy consumption, and restoring the existing Everglades wetlands. The resulting complex form of the glass building enclosure and exterior sunshades required a finely calibrated, multi-step process across various tools and media. In addition to the commonly understood technical workflow, the firm recognised the importance of strategic and tactical workflows.

Long before the architects were hired, a strategic workflow was at play. A bridging/design-build project delivery method was implemented to assure the government's need for quality, cost and schedule outcomes was met. Analogous to an hourglass, this workflow was purposefully pinched at the moment of design handover to the contracting team.

Two narrow office wings were massed to respond to functional needs and to provide a dynamic response to the organic natural environment. The technical workflow to develop the curved and folded curtain-wall geometries oscillated between conceptual form-finding, virtual architectural modelling, environmental performance analysis, physical modelling through 3D printing, geometry and panel optimisation, mock-up production and testing, and final fabrication and installation.

Tactical workflow, as Krueck + Sexton came to realise, is arguably the most important of the three, underpinning both technical and strategic workflows. By its very nature, workflow is dependent upon a successful interaction between a sender and receiver who exchange information. What makes the interaction effective is not just when the content is sent and received, but when a shared interpretation of the meaning and implications can be ascertained. In this way, workflow primarily depends on good communication.

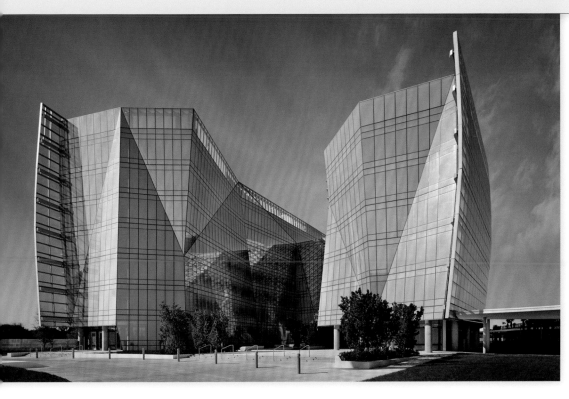

The two office building wings enclose and shade the entry courtyard. Visitors and federal agents experience a comfortable arrival sequence that is defined by a gradual transition from an outside to inside climate.

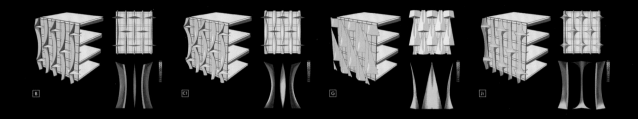

Early Simulation and Testing Workflows

In designing the United States Embassy in London (2016), KieranTimberlake sought to embrace the core democratic values of transparency, openness and equality while also meeting the ambitious security, sustainability and programming goals of a diplomatic building. One of the building's signature features is its multilayered envelope made of a lightweight, extruded aluminium frame and tensioned ethylene tetrafluoroethylene (ETFE). Because it is a highly transparent, UV-stable polymer, the ETFE allows the envelope to modulate incident solar radiation in order to minimise the building's mechanical systems design and simultaneously provide daylight and manage glare. These unique benefits reduce electrical lighting demands and ensure a comfortable working environment while also meeting security and weather protection standards.

The team was intrigued by tensile structures because of their light weight and the opportunity they provide for creating performative, multidirectional facades. However, the designers' limited experience working with ETFE meant they had to gain a deeper understanding of the material's properties and potential for balancing design and performance demands before they could move from concept to reality. Supported by Arup facade engineers, the architects created initial form studies in Rhino and Autodesk® Revit, but found that neither program could simulate ETFE's natural behaviour, possible geometry or reactions to being stretched and deformed while under stress. KieranTimberlake therefore made iterative physical models, sewed and pulled material to measure its tensile behaviour, and deployed computational tools that analysed and tweaked shapes in order to visualise surface tension and illustrate how material stresses influence performance.

To arrive at an optimal shape for individual ETFE forms, the team used Rhino3D® and custom Grasshopper™ scripts to analyse curvature in both principal directions to achieve uniform stress distribution over the anticlastic form.

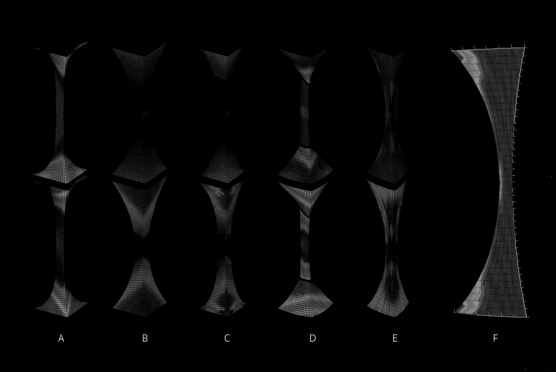

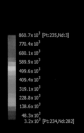

860.7 x 10³ [Pt:235,Nd:3]
770.4 x 10³
680.1 x 10³
589.9 x 10³
499.6 x 10³
409.4 x 10³
319.1 x 10³
228.8 x 10³
138.6 x 10³
48.3 x 10³
3.2 x 10³ [Pt:234,Nd:282]

A   B   C   D   E   F

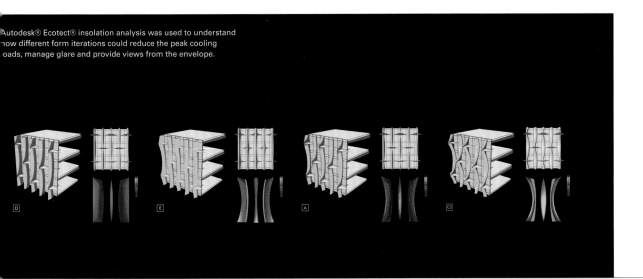

Autodesk® Ecotect® insolation analysis was used to understand how different form iterations could reduce the peak cooling loads, manage glare and provide views from the envelope.

The designers used feedback from custom computational tools and tensile membrane design software, including Rhino® Membrane (now a Grasshopper™ plugin) and Mehler® TensileDraw, to test different shapes. From there, Autodesk's Ecotect Analysis was used to quantify incident solar radiation and daylighting in occupied spaces. Zeroing-in on how the sun would pass through a space over time, the architects determined areas where glare or heat gain might be a problem, and tuned the facade geometry and interior layout so that occupants sitting near the perimeter would be properly shaded. Simultaneously, Arup panellised the geometry of the outer envelope and ran high-fidelity radiance models to verify the geometry, structural efficiencies and solar performance of the facade.

In addition to smaller-scale models and computational tools, full-scale prototypes built with the facade's actual materials were used to understand how ETFE behaved on a structural frame. Creating a feedback loop between a two-storey model unit component and the full building facade, computational scripts were built for aggregating and translating the performance metrics of different combinations and orientations. This feedback loop helped the team to zero-in on ideal locations for the envelope's apertures that would optimise daylighting, views and shading while minimising incident solar radiation. Additionally, the iterative process and use of custom tools allowed the streamlining of informational hand-offs between the KieranTimberlake and Arup offices.

By implementing a workflow that involved early simulation and testing with a diverse toolset, the design team was able to cast a wide net, working iteratively to understand the potential and development of the concept in profound ways. The expanded involvement of consultants and fabricators allowed the multivariant process to unfold and ultimately produce a more elegant and performative envelope.

Exterior rendering of the embassy featuring the ETFE forms.

LMN Architects,
School of Music Building,
University of Iowa,
Iowa City,
2016

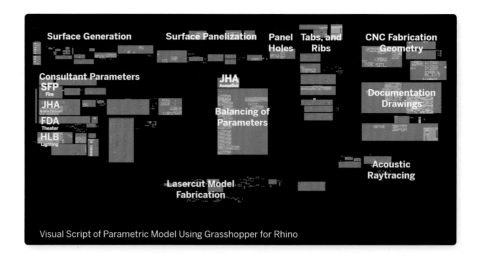

Visual Script of Parametric Model Using Grasshopper for Rhino

Direct-to-Fabrication Workflows

An emerging workflow that changed the way LMN Architects practices began with the new School of Music Building for the University of Iowa (2016). Buildings designed for the celebration and enjoyment of live music are complicated: issues of acoustic performance, sound transmittance, lighting and life safety are all critical elements of the building's success, as well as the architectural quality of space, light and craft that is expected of such venues. For the Iowa building, these challenges were augmented by the requirement to deliver the project in a low-bid procurement environment, meaning that LMN's preferred method of early collaboration with fabricators would be impossible. This is where many designers stay conservative and build within established means, selecting systems and finishes from catalogues and well-known methods

of construction. However, LMN's team took a different route, choosing instead to test their capacities in developing bespoke design solutions and using direct-to-fabrication methods to prove their viability.

The theatroacoustic high-performance ceiling system for the main concert hall was developed to accommodate a host of technical needs within a graceful form that encloses the space. LMN created a robust parametric digital model in Grasshopper that coordinated and rationalised a host of data inputs from structural, theatrical, lighting, acoustic and fire-protection consultants. The challenge was to make these disparate elements work together and to unify them within a single system, ensuring that the unique result would not only be aesthetically pleasing, but realistically buildable within a low-bid 2D document process.

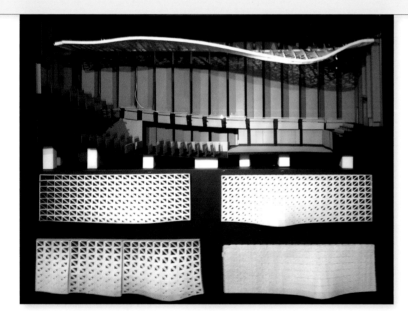

Prototyping was a part of the process from the earliest studies, providing a chance to refine the direct-to-fabrication process for collaboration among the consultant team.

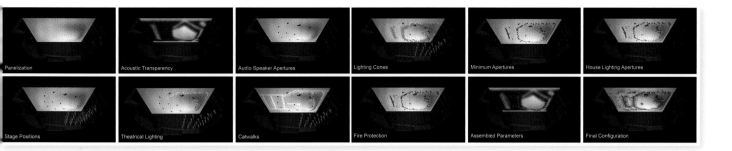

| Panelization | Acoustic Transparency | Audio Speaker Apertures | Lighting Cones | Minimum Apertures | House Lighting Apertures |
| Stage Positions | Theatrical Lighting | Catwalks | Fire Protection | Assembled Parameters | Final Configuration |

As the Grasshopper model synthesised the evolving inputs and parameters, the team also explored the formal evolution through 3D physical models. These models became important collaborative tools, allowing the various consultants to interact with the form in a collaborative setting and simultaneously forcing the designers to refine the process of outputting fabrication data for the panellised system. While the jump in scale to the full-size system would be significant, the methods of deriving the data to fabricate the elements would be virtually the same.

This physical engagement with the developing idea became a crucial new step in LMN's process. They speculated that a unique material could be used for the application – composite aluminium panel, developed as a cost-effective facade cladding for buildings, and their in-house CNC mill became an invaluable resource for fabricating full-size panel prototypes and a constructed mock-up. These assets were important for proving the viability of the system to the project stakeholders while simultaneously allowing the design team to validate construction detailing and assembly sequencing with their own hands.

The knowledge gained from this process was thus an essential part of the project's documentation and successful bidding. Diagrams and schedules in the documents indicated the level of complexity achievable only with direct-to-fabrication technology, and a schedule of panel dimensions was published to prove that the data to fabricate the system existed. The strategy worked, and the winning bidder used LMN's model to directly fabricate the installed product.

left and opening spread: The final suspended theatroacoustic system installed, shown here during construction.

Technical Innovation and Social Dynamics

For SOM's Seattle-Tacoma (Sea-Tac) International Airport expansion project, due to be completed in 2019, success depended on completion of construction in the shortest amount of time with minimal impact on airport operations, level of service and safety. Working within the overlapping design and construction phases required by a progressive design-build delivery method meant that coordination with the project stakeholders, airport users, operations and other capital projects was of utmost importance. The design took place in the same physical space as Clark Construction, which was pricing the parts and construction cost of SOM's schemes. The fast-tracked project pushed the SOM team to evolve a design workflow into something more versatile and flexible than its designers were accustomed to.

The subtle double-curvature in the new International Arrivals Facility building's sinuous massing might not look daunting, but the quick pace of the project posed challenges to SOM's usual methodology of using the best tool for the specific problem and developing custom solutions to connect data among various tools. Working with Autodesk Revit to coordinate the different trades and produce the contract documents, the customary process for exploring complex geometric options has been to begin with parametric studies in Grasshopper and Rhino before exporting the digested geometry to adaptive components in Revit for documentation. This linear one-way workflow is common in complex geometry projects, and SOM has used various combinations of tools developed for this specific purpose: Hummingbird, Lyrebird, GeometryGym, MantaShrimp, Grevit, Rhynamo,

Along with its continuous undulating roof, the fluid form of the new International Arrivals Facility building is defined by a desire to preserve views to existing architecture, provide passengers with ample natural daylight and uninterrupted lines of sight, as well as functional requirements such as standoff distance to an elevated light rail and future access road.

A 235-metre (770-foot) walkway provides connection between the existing south satellite and the International Arrivals Facility via a sterile circulation path over the existing taxi lane. The design is the result of synthesising an opportunity for expansive views of the surrounding Pacific Northwest landscape for the arriving international passengers while respecting aircraft standoff distances, maintaining functional widths for optimal passenger flow, fire and life safety, and maximising the efficient use of space and materials.

as well as its own internally developed tools. Once imported into Revit, the geometries become hosts to Revit elements (including construction-level details, dimensions and other annotations) that perish once the hosting geometries need to be updated, requiring repetitive work. For typically paced projects, this loss and rework is a begrudgingly accepted workflow within the design team.

However, SOM's Sea-Tac expansion designs were developed into construction-level detail from the early phases, so not having the persistence of these Revit elements on the host geometry was not acceptable. After numerous variations of the one-way workflow were explored, a solution to complete the iterative cycle began to emerge, accomplished by storing the Revit element IDs, as well as the defining geometrical parameters, and exchanging this information with Grasshopper via comma-separated values (CSV) files. Once the Revit geometry is edited in Grasshopper, the information in CSV format is similarly read back into Revit through Dynamo.

The first generation of this solution may be an acute one developed for the particular parameters relevant to the geometries in the Sea-Tac project, but its growth into a more robust solution is imminent. A working example such as this spawns new ideas among those invested in the process of how things are done, once again underlining the importance of embedded project experience for the most relevant computation innovation in architecture. The true value of workflows lies not only in technical innovation, but also in the ways in which they allow designers to nimbly respond to the challenging social dynamics of projects.

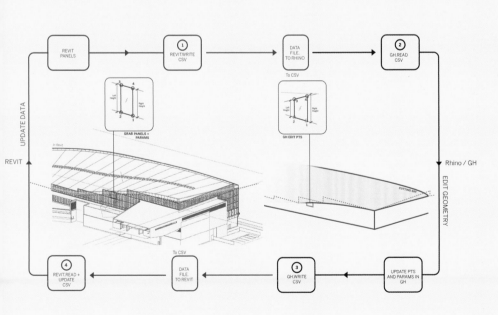

A two-way exchange of data between Grasshopper/Rhino and Dynamo/Revit via custom components addresses a much-needed completion of the iterative loop in the design and documentation process. Many designers generating complex geometry still prefer not to model them natively in Dynamo/Revit and will continue to persist for many reasons, making interoperability a very relevant part of the single-source-model conversations surrounding the ideal BIM process.

Populous,
Jacksonville Jaguars
Amphitheater and
Training Facility,
Jacksonville,
Florida,
2017

The new Jacksonville Jaguars Amphitheater and Training Facility is enclosed by a dynamic roofscape, providing the new state-of-the-art facility with a unique architectural expression that further activates the city's riverfront walk adjacent to the St Johns River.

Populous's design process for the Jacksonville Jaguars Amphitheater and Training Facility in Florida was made possible through integrated design and fabrication modelling.

Non-Conventional Workflows Determined by Time Constraints

Populous's design process for the Jacksonville Jaguars Amphitheater and Training Facility in Florida (due to open in June 2017; see p 70) was made possible through integrated design and fabrication modelling.

The Jaguars approached Populous in November 2015 to deliver an iconic architectural design solution to service two new programmes to be located outside its existing home at Everbank Field: an amphitheatre for the Jacksonville community, and a training facility for the football team. The greatest challenge was an extremely aggressive schedule. With substantial completion scheduled for April 2017, the project team implemented a non-conventional workflow to initiate an early start to fabrication-phase modelling, which would typically occur post-award of the contract for construction. Project structural engineers Walter P Moore not only delivered design information to Populous, but initiated the structural steel connection design, including bolted and welded connections and gusset plates required for the attachment of members – all accomplished prior to

completion of the contract documents and execution of the contract for construction between the owner and builder. Under standard project delivery, connection design would normally be provided by the structural steel contractor. In this case, this work was to be performed by the project's structural engineers, enabling the team to meet the aggressive schedule.

The associated risks imposed on a project team where a separate entity provides services for the architect and the contractor, can only be navigated with clear and highly defined scopes of work and an understanding of when and for whom the scope is provided. Such was the case for the structural steel work for the Jacksonville Jaguars project, where the connection design and fabrication phase modelling clearly came under the contractor's scope of work. The point of award for the contract, in this instance, fell between the connection design and fabrication modelling efforts. While connection design ultimately became the responsibility of the steel contractor, fabrication modeling was performed directly for the fabricator under separate contract with the structural engineers.

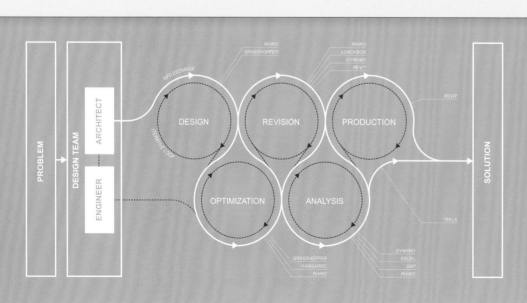

Strong interdependency and collaboration between the architects and structural engineers was developed to build an efficient and iterative workflow throughout all phases of the project, including design, optimisation, revision, analysis and production.

Explaining Workflows

The five projects illustrated here, while all different, began in the same place: with a question. The best way to expose what had been until now hidden in the built form is by thoughtfully determining the questions we ask. To better explain workflows, it is necessary to start with better questions; those individuals and firms should be asking now to determine how projects are accomplished. These might include: What percentage of the firm's workflows are similar from project to project, and what portion are custom designed? What workflows were unique to this project? Comparing the architects' project workflow(s) with those from 10 to 15 years ago, what remains the same, and what has changed? What overriding criteria are used to determine a workflow? What end goals did the architects' custom workflows have on the project? Were they more practical outcomes (faster/better/cheaper), or were there more expansive goals? What are some of the custom tools and/or work processes the firm introduced into the project design process, and during construction?

In addition, how does a firm decide that a custom tool needs to be innovated at a particular time in the design process? What does that process and series of decisions look like? How important is it that some of the other team members outside the architectural firm – consultants, tradespersons, engineers – are familiar with the architects' work processes?

Architects can think of these questions as a lens through which to see current projects, as well as an opportunity to scrutinise – and improve upon – the effectiveness of those that are already completed. By starting with questions, they will be able to better understand and explain their own workflows, as well as those of others. ᴆ

The author would like to thank Tom Jacobs of Krueck + Sexton Architects, Sejung Kat Park of SOM, Jonathan Mallie of Populous, Stephen van Dyck of LMN, and Matthew Krissel, Mark Davis and Carin Whitney of KierenTimberlake for their contributions to this article.

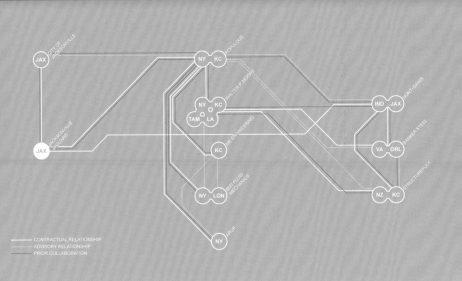

Team collaboration was challenged by distance between various office locations across the country. However, pre-existing and developing working relationships served as a catalyst in maximising the benefits of collaborative design.

Jonathan Mallie

Expansive Workflows

Downstream Coordination
in the Design of Sporting
Facilities

Populous,
Bristol Arena,
Bristol,
UK,
due for completion 2018

left: Populous designed the Bristol Arena to deliver a world-class live music venue for 12,000 fans while creating a vibrant new quarter in the city. Citing Bristol's position as 2015's European Green Capital, the design team hopes to achieve a BREEAM 'Excellent' rating, which will make it the UK's most sustainable arena when it opens in 2018.

Heightening user experience is a key aim for global architecture practice Populous, specialists in designing sports and entertainment venues. **Jonathan Mallie**, lead principal in their New York office, outlines their working process. The digital realm plays an important part: from building information modelling, to immersive technologies that imaginatively engage communities in the creative process. But such large-scale, time-sensitive projects as the Jacksonville Jaguars American football facility in Florida would be impossible without also establishing a team spirit among all those involved.

Populous,
Philippine Arena,
Manila,
Philippines,
2014

The world's largest mixed-use indoor theatre has seating for 50,000 and a landscaped exterior that can accommodate an additional 50,000 people. It supports major church gatherings and also serves as a multi-use sports and concert venue, hosting a range of events from boxing and basketball to live music performances.

Over the last three decades, Populous has designed sports and entertainment venues that have brought people together all over the world. While the firm's core work remains in these building types, it also provides a wide range of other services, and through its architecture, interiors, planning and brand activation takes a holistic approach to enriching user experience. In imagining spaces where large numbers of people gather, this drives many of the design decisions that go into such complex structures.

The international aspect of the firm's work has had a profound effect on its design approach. Populous has an extensive understanding of how various cultures respond to its projects, and can therefore deliver highly informed design anywhere around the globe. In the case of sports architecture, factors here might be cultural differences in the way sports are played and viewed, and fan expectations before, during and after the game, which enable Populous to create exceptional experiences across multiple building types while leveraging technology and data to inform the design.

When starting a project, the design team engages the surrounding community and local stakeholders with a series of questions as a way to understand how to heighten user experience through the activation of interior and exterior spaces throughout a sporting season. Such an experience contributes to the brand and identity of the complex. Increasingly, the firm relies on immersive technologies that brings participants closer to the physical environment of play. The aim is to design experiences for people.

Populous,
Jacksonville Jaguars Amphitheater and Training Facility,
Jacksonville,
Florida,
2017

below and bottom: The proposed architectural solution imagined the amphitheatre and training centre as a connective membrane between EverBank Field and the developing riverfront district, which spans from the stadium towards the southern edge of the site. Its southern facade affronts the expressway and waterfront, evoking a sense of movement towards future riverfront development.

Sporting venue owners often make commitments to their home cities and fan bases that their teams will, for example, play on opening day. Populous's projects must therefore invariably be completed within a precisely scheduled period of time and by a particular date. There is no room for delays nor opportunities to 'push the schedule out' by a season or two, either when building a new venue or renovating an existing one. Fixed event dates thus become key in the establishment of constraint-based design criteria and the creation of a digitally influenced building design and delivery workflow.

This workflow was developed by Populous in response to what are often unforgiving design schedules that only allow for real-time adjustments in order to keep pace with critical project milestones.

Collaboration and Digital Delivery Through Workflows

The firm's designers are continually looking for ways to further integrate the design and construction process in their work. This includes optimising information from digital design models to expedite the traditional shop drawing process and achieve new levels of efficiency and accuracy in the architectural workflow that support the complexities of large-scale venues.

In many cases, the structural system for a sporting venue is long-span structural steel. This is a key aspect of arena design that needs to be resolved by the architects and structural engineers prior to completion of the design phases, and relies on early procurement and completion of construction documentation packages. Building owners must therefore commit to making timely and informed decisions, and the design team must undertake to streamline the workflow of information to advance drawing packages with confidence that the design will not undergo significant change. Decision matrices and the information needed from each consultant require careful coordination among design team members to establish workflow efficiency.

In recent projects, including Jacksonville Jaguars Amphitheater and Training Facility, Populous is increasingly mixing hospitality and commercial programmes with sporting and live performance facilities. In these cases, performative and technical characteristics influencing geometric rationalisation and form, and the digital workflow developed for the design and construction phases, require a pliant software platform that relies heavily on the programming of various parametric tools such as Grasshopper and Dynamo to regenerate the digital geometry. This automated and iterative process means that Populous does not have to remodel multiple versions of the project in order to test efficiencies. Grasshopper permits parametric geometric development while Dynamo enables the seamless transfer of geometry between Rhino and Revit for production of the construction documents. This workflow was developed by Populous in response to what are often unforgiving design schedules that only allow for real-time adjustments in order to keep pace with critical project milestones.

To this end, Populous believes that construction teams should be engaged, whenever possible, at the schematic design stage of a project. With the right construction-side partner, invaluable information can be obtained and incorporated throughout the design process. Digital building information modelling (BIM) is the vehicle through which both design and construction data flows between the project team members. When properly utilised, workflow efficiency is increased, and unnecessary value engineering exercises are avoided since cost optimisation is also controlled within the BIM.

A Performative Design Approach

Inspired by the city's vast network of estuaries and steel bridges that span the St Johns River, for the Jacksonville Jaguars Amphitheater and Training Facility, next to the football team's playing field in Jacksonville, Florida, Populous conceived a dynamic undulating roofscape to canvas the two new programmes, providing a state-of-the-art facility for both public and private events with a unique architectural expression and form.

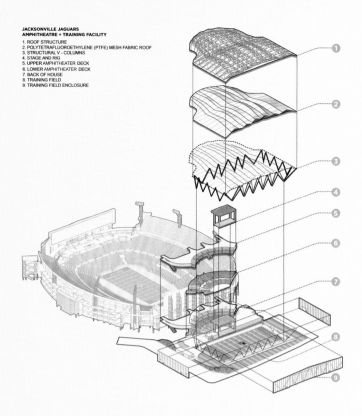

JACKSONVILLE JAGUARS
AMPHITHEATRE + TRAINING FACILITY

1. ROOF STRUCTURE
2. POLYTETRAFLUOROETHLYLENE (PTFE) MESH FABRIC ROOF
3. STRUCTURAL V - COLUMNS
4. STAGE AND RIG
5. UPPER AMPHITHEATER DECK
6. LOWER AMPHITHEATER DECK
7. BACK OF HOUSE
8. TRAINING FIELD
9. TRAINING FIELD ENCLOSURE

Populous,
Jacksonville Jaguars Amphitheater and Training Facility,
Jacksonville,
Florida,
2017

above: Exploded axonometric of the building components.

below: Custom Grasshopper™ scripts were developed in order to embed performative design criteria into the digital design process. The roof membrane was treated as a parametric surface that responded to a series of inputs that influenced the final form.

Due to open in June 2017, more than 80 per cent of the project's building materials are fabric and steel. The undulating form of the roofscape is constrained through the use of a polytetrafluoroethylene (PTFE) fabric suspended from a series of planar steel trusses. Each truss is oriented north–south and spans 130 metres (430 feet) from the southern end of the stadium to the southern facade of the training facility. The trusses are loaded onto an array of structural steel V-columns, which delicately support the fabric roof above.

With the benefits of parametric design extending beyond digital coordination and rationalisation, Populous and BMT Fluid Mechanics incorporated performance-based design criteria such as drainage, lighting, natural ventilation and the structural properties of the fabric and steel components into the digital design model using digital simulation processes. The articulation of the roof geometry took advantage of a 'peak and valley' deployment of the fabric material, driven by the shape of each longitudinal truss and its vertical distance from the ground, thus dictating the drainage pattern. Here, rather than allowing performative criteria to hinder the development of architectural form, it was used to rationalise it, allowing the building's expression to become a manifestation of its efficiency.

Architects typically deliver a geometric design proposal to a project's structural engineers, who in turn develop a structural solution for the building. In the case of the Jacksonville Jaguars project, however, Populous's goal to house multiple programmes under a singular, column-free space called for early input of the structural design criteria for the steel trusses and the fabric roof. The fabric roof was panellised, maximising the number of panels that exceeded 65 square metres (700 square feet) to avoid excessive wind pressures. This became a guiding principle for the early

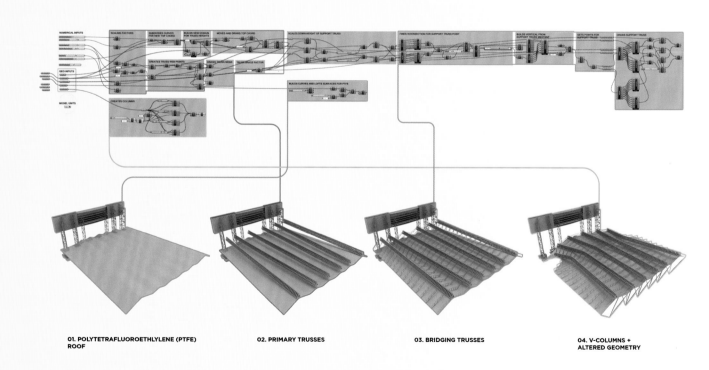

01. POLYTETRAFLUOROETHLYLENE (PTFE) ROOF

02. PRIMARY TRUSSES

03. BRIDGING TRUSSES

04. V-COLUMNS + ALTERED GEOMETRY

development of the roof geometry in terms of relative position over the programme, including the height requirements imposed by the structural steel rig over the performance stage, and the appropriate mid-field height of the training facility to allow for the clearance necessary for punting a football.

Integrated Design and Construction

The owner's selection of Hunt Construction Group as construction manager for the project completed the owner-architect-contractor partnership, while also maintaining the ability to leverage the pre-existing working relationships within the design team. This was essential to ensure collaboration in arriving at a guaranteed maximum price (GMP) for construction. The collaborative efforts of the designers were also improved with the addition of Hunt, whose initiatives to reach out to the market, solicit interest and pricing from the subcontracting community, and lead a design-assist engagement with key subcontractors was the only way the iconic project could be completed on time and for the stated budget.

During the construction-manager-led design-assist stage, Populous developed a highly unique workflow that enabled a seamless and exponential flow of information between the design model and construction-phase fabrication models. Typically, fabrication modelling would occur post-completion of the design documents and subsequent award of the project to the builder. In this case, however, the integrated design and construction team instituted a workflow that authorised development of the fabrication model based on input gathered from the design-assist contractors prior to the completion of the contract documents and agreement on the GMP.

From specific design-phase parametric modelling to construction-phase fabrication modelling, the development of the Jacksonville project was possible only through the integrated approach of the team, including the venue owner, who played a critical role in providing timely decisions and feedback in order to keep the project on track. Regardless of increasingly robust digital toolsets, working relationships fostered and maintained through the design and delivery workflow are critical to the realisation of such ambitious projects. As with many Populous buildings, for the Jacksonville Jaguars Amphitheater and Training Facility, communication, collaboration and trust once again served as the crucial factors in determining the ultimate success of the project. ∆

bottom: The building will feature a 5,500-seat amphitheatre and 8,730-square-metre (94,000-square-foot) multi-use indoor facility for team practice. It is anticipated that once opened, the facility will bring the annual National Football League (NFL) Draft to Jacksonville.

below: Connection detailing and engineering of the primary structure began prior to the awarding of the steel contract in order to resolve complex conditions, assure integration with the enclosure strategy and control aesthetics and cost.

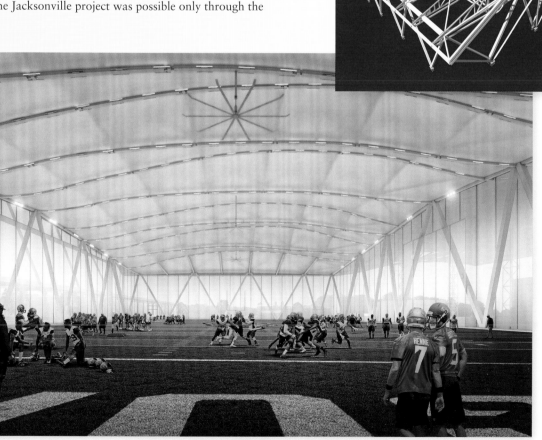

From Pencils to Partners

The Next Role of Computation in Building Design

As building information modelling (BIM) software becomes ever more powerful, how will the architect's role be affected? **Ian Keough and Anthony Hauck** of the AEC Generative Design group at leading software corporation Autodesk present their vision. They argue that the value of building professionals' expertise in advising clients on priorities and choices has never been higher. BIM offers greater guarantees of structural integrity and constructional feasibility, and scalable cloud computing allows numerous factors to be explored simultaneously; but success is only assured if the right parameters are set.

While it is tempting to declare that the introduction of information technology over the last 40 years has irrevocably changed the professions of building design and construction, we may instead be returning to a more traditional engagement with the built environment, supported by the very technologies often cited as agents of profound change.

Since the first recognised need for constructed shelter there have been goals, requirements and constraints driving building decisions, with the skills of builders primarily determining the relative success of the results. Buildings have always been evaluated according to their basic provision of comfort, but sometimes with an even higher regard for their aesthetic effects on the inhabitants; there are numerous leaky buildings that remain widely admired for their instantiation of form and their modulations of space and light. While the details of professional practice in building design and construction have certainly evolved with the wide availability of powerful computation, the goals of commodity, firmness and delight remain constant, the requirements of individual projects must be considered, and the constraints of available budget, schedule, site, materials and skills must still be addressed.

From Pencils to Pixels
Buildings predate the drawing conventions with which the modern building industry is familiar, but it was professional drafting, not building, that was served by the earliest computer-aided design (CAD) products and their ubiquitous successors such as Autodesk's AutoCAD, Bentley's MicroStation and Nemetschek's Vectorworks. It should be no surprise that the earliest intersection of comparatively limited computing capabilities and building design and construction practice targeted the most tractable problem in the industry: graphically recording and conveying building decisions. The visual conventions of construction drafting and rendering had been largely settled for more than a century when CAD became widely available, affording a professional culture that recognised efficient drafting and realistic rendering as two obvious and urgent needs that could be satisfied by limited computational enhancement. Other common design and construction problems such as drawing coordination and consistency checking remained exercises little different from the days of ink on linen.

From Pixels to Parameters
With the advent of building information modelling (BIM), the building professions began to realise possibilities for greater computational involvement in the design and construction process, relegating traditional drafting and drawing coordination to side benefits of modelling the project. BIM instantiated a metaphor of the building process derived from the procedures of the manufacturing sector, treating the

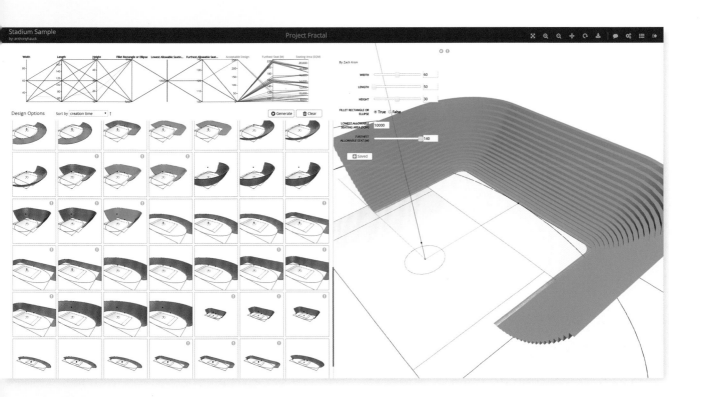

Autodesk, Stadium seating study, Project Fractal, 2016

Autodesk's Project Fractal displays a series of options for stadium seating derived from
the scalable computation of a generative and evaluative Dynamo Studio graph.

building as an emergent phenomenon that arises from the assembly of virtual components maintaining specific spatial and behavioural relationships. The approach has reliably deepened and accelerated the prospective understanding of a building's design; subsequent advances on the basis of BIM technology have increased confidence in predictions of a building's fitness, with the highest confidence attaching to critical analyses of structural integrity and mechanical system performance.

While the convenience and accuracy of these evaluations are well established, such uses of BIM are merely digital recapitulations of approaches that once depended for success on a builder's experienced intuition or the explicit mathematical expression of fundamental physical principles. Computation has facilitated the dissemination of the building professions' current state of the art, but its limited capacity has also limited its ability to help designers, builders and clients determine what should be built.

Through the agency of businesses such as Amazon Web Services and Microsoft Azure, and natively developed corporate capabilities, scalable computation has become widely available. This has given rise to reliable video-streaming services such as Netflix, specialist software services offered by companies such as Salesforce, Adobe and Autodesk, and the ubiquity of highly functional mobile

applications depending on scalable computation to offer functionality once only available on desktop computers. Accessible computation has become effectively infinite, with the ability to enlist arbitrary quantities of computers to explore many aspects of a design problem simultaneously.

Under these new conditions, computation can support the actual design and construction process by providing a more complete understanding of a choice's consequences in the context of many possible alternatives. With the capability of wider design exploration, a building's constituents can recognise their true goals and requirements while prioritising their needs in the context of the project's constraints. The confrontation by a designer of a blank screen as a visual analogue to a blank drafting sheet will seem as antiquated to future professionals as linen and T-squares have become to the building professions today. As technology companies take advantage of scalable computation and ubiquitous public information, physical context and regulatory constraint will become inherent characteristics of project design, with professionals introducing particular goals and requirements and aiding clients to prioritise their needs.

Where CAD and BIM have advanced the ability to record design and construction intent more accurately and consistently, in the latter case helping to advance the understanding of prospective building performance more

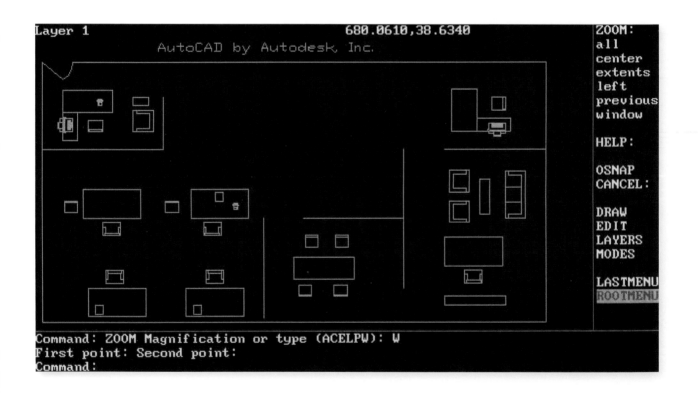

Autodesk, Example office plan, Autodesk AutoCAD, 1985

In the early days of CAD on personal computers, simple vector graphics began
replacing physical drafting by translating architectural drawing conventions into
computing environments, addressing issues of dimensional accuracy and consistency
without examining broader design coordination issues.

intuitively, the ability to record the logic leading to design and construction decisions has also advanced with the availability of visual programming environments related to the increasingly widespread use of parameterisation in the manufacturing and building professions. Environments such as Robert McNeel & Associates' Grasshopper and Autodesk's Dynamo Studio afford visual metaphors that can help capture goals, requirements and constraints, using those parameters to propose solutions for discrete or holistic building problems.

The inclusion of fabrication methods and construction logic in design decisions will become routine and repeatable as more building knowledge is captured and delivered through scalable cloud services created by design and construction firms and offered on contract to projects. Milestone-checking protocols will become quaint recollections because digital environments supporting building design and construction will be inherently and constantly evaluating a project's representation against its recorded goals, requirements and constraints, guiding professionals toward promising solutions.

From Parameters to Practice

Architecture, engineering and construction (AEC) industry practice is poised to return to a deep intertwining of intent, fabrication and construction methodologies

> The inclusion of fabrication methods and construction logic in design decisions will become routine and repeatable as more building knowledge is captured and delivered through scalable cloud services created by design and construction firms

Autodesk, Example hospital model, 2016

Sophisticated building information modelling provided building professionals with the ability to spatially coordinate multiple intersecting systems, employ prospective analysis of behaviour and derive construction documentation from recorded design decisions.

uncommon since the Renaissance, with professional tools encompassing the capture and repeatable delivery of contextually relevant building knowledge and expertise. Current professional practice still harkens back to the earliest days of building, with design, construction and operational building performance highly dependent on the skills of the individual professionals assigned the work. Emerging computational and knowledge delivery systems are beginning to forge new environments offering the promise of optimised building performance more dependent on professional and client prioritisation than on the serendipitous assignment to projects of perfectly trained and appropriately experienced teams of building experts working in concert with sophisticated clients. Employing scalable computation and cloud data systems, building design and construction firms have an opportunity to expand their influence into many more projects than are currently supportable with finite consulting capacity. Services created by encoding professional expertise could provide new forms of consultation through captured knowledge and generative algorithms employing machine learning to constantly improve the quality of solution proposals.

Clarifying building requirements and project constraints while evaluating proposed solutions in response to client aspirations will become the recognised benefits

Current professional practice still harkens back to the earliest days of building, with design, construction and operational building performance highly dependent on the skills of the individual professionals assigned the work.

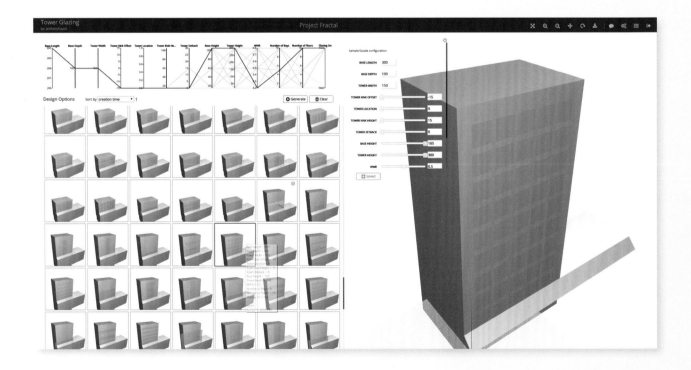

Autodesk, Building envelope study, Project Fractal, 2016

Autodesk's Project Fractal is a web application that generates multiple design proposals from a single Dynamo Studio graph, cycling through multiple configurations of designated factors influencing the design. The parallel coordinates graph describes the variables and outcomes of a selected design, each of which can be individually edited by changing the inputs of the graph.

of professional involvement in projects, with much of the current necessary research into contextual conditions and regulatory environments relegated to automated delivery and project inclusion through contracted web services. Project requirements will become statements of desire for architectural functions of specified capacity, with professional intervention required to choose from the many possible solutions computationally generated in response to project conditions and in service to project goals. Far from diminishing the importance of the building professions, scalable computation will highlight their unique value in guiding clients toward what should be built, with the manifest support of the relevant data and discernible logic leading to proposed solutions of evident functionality, regulatory compliance and aesthetic merit.

Autodesk's Project Fractal, which began development in November 2015 and entered public alpha testing in July 2016, is created as an open system applicable to multiple design problems, employing scalable cloud computation to generate proposals while facilitating rapid evaluation of those solutions. High-performing design candidates assessed by custom evaluators can be selected for further exploration and elaboration. While such tools have been developed and explored in a number of academic institutions and professional firms for decades, the availability of cloud computing now affords the AEC industry

the opportunity and academia to accelerate more widely its computational delivery of professional expertise and the advancement of building design, construction and operations in conjunction with academic investigations.

Where design and construction firms may invest considerably in the study of a few alternative designs or construction approaches, Project Fractal's use of scalable computation allows the designer to range more widely through possible solutions generatively produced, prompting further exploration along avenues previously deemed impractical due to aggressive schedules and fee constraints. By employing generative and analytical techniques, designers and builders can quickly evaluate an extensive array of alternatives for a critical building decision.

Autodesk's collaboration with healthcare planners at architecture firm Perkins+Will in January–August 2016 resulted in the prototype Space Plan Generator graph in Autodesk® Dynamo Studio that accounts for a number of key goals, requirements and constraints applicable to a hospital-bed tower project. Incorporated evaluation functions indicate to the designer the relative success of each proposal linearly generated from manipulations of input factors. Submitting the graph to Project Fractal creates multiple plan alternatives generated from varying combinations of key parameters for comparison by the designer both visually and through identified metrics.

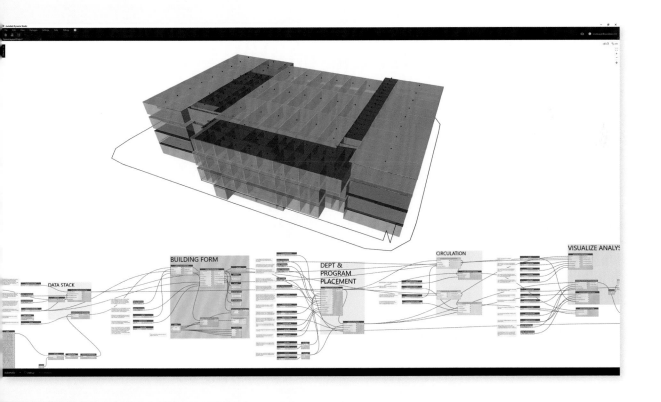

Autodesk and Perkins+Will, Space Plan Generator graph,
Autodesk Dynamo Studio, 2016

Autodesk's Space Plan Generator was developed in Dynamo Studio from January to August 2016 in conjunction with healthcare planners at Perkins+Will's Atlanta, Georgia office. The graph accepts input of a tabular space programming document and a site boundary to propose functional space plans for multiple floors of this test project.

Beyond design and construction process authorship, designers will also increasingly author building decision systems

From Practice to Partners

From Practice to Partners

Beyond design and construction process authorship, designers will also increasingly author building decision systems, encoding their unique workflows, perspectives and expertise into procedures that preserve and extend their approaches more reliably for more projects into which they, or their authored services, are contracted. Expertise that had only been applicable to a few projects at once, given limits of professional availability, will be scalable to an arbitrary number of projects, informing and guiding project teams and their clients to superior solutions. Building professionals will orchestrate and prioritise services as well as the contribution of other team members to deliver the best value for clients and the public. They will be appropriately balancing conflicting needs and more narrowly optimised solutions with contextual judgement while considering a wider variety of analytically evaluated alternatives than previously considered practical.

A subsequent investigation using Project Fractal begun in May 2016 applies a similar approach to building facades, with alternatives generated by computationally varying the quantity of fenestration bays, the degree of shading and the physical appearance of the shading devices. Even within a narrowed acceptable performance range, a wide variety of architectural alternatives can be rapidly considered, guiding the professional toward a decision, the consequences of which can be understood in the context of the project's requirements.

As delivery of expertise through scalable computation and data availability becomes commonplace, firms that once differentiated on technological advantage will begin to differentiate in areas to which they have often aspired – on their unique perspective and judgement, as represented both by their current staff and their computationally delivered expertise. Having begun in the province of organisational culture and professional mentorship, the

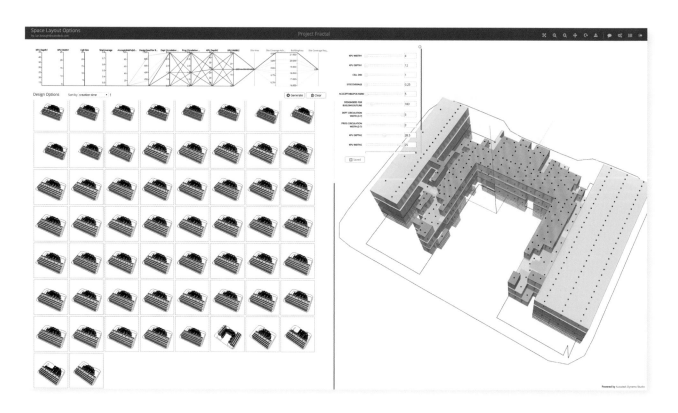

Autodesk and Perkins+Will, Space Plan studies, Project Fractal, 2016

The Space Plan Generator graph submitted from Dynamo Studio to Project Fractal produces multiple options for a hospital-bed tower within a supplied site boundary. Following a hierarchy of space placement described in a tabular space programme document, the Space Plan Generator distributes spaces to arrive at floor plate, adjacency, and area allocations as constrained by a specified site coverage percentage.

industry's standard of care will also become reliant on the continual enhancement and experience of generative design systems whose improvement will be guided by successive generations of professionals and the state of the art in the building industry. Far from dependence on a fortunate encounter with the right information at the right time, computationally scalable building systems will become invaluable and ubiquitous differentiating tools implementing and applying historical and situational organisational expertise.

Technology providers will similarly evolve to support an ecosystem of services for the building design and construction industries. Just as systems of physical transport and energy delivery support efficient and profitable commerce, software providers will offer the means to record and deliver building expertise to the right constituencies at the right time, improving outcomes for clients and allowing professionals to scale their practices both geographically and for a wider variety of project types. Firms will draw upon available computationally delivered expertise to compete more effectively by enhancing and extending their native skills. Software providers will accelerate the development and delivery of each professional's unique contributions, offering geometric authoring and computational environments that support projects optimised to satisfy client goals

while acknowledging functional requirements and project constraints. With a sufficient computational and service infrastructure, the building professions can focus on developing and providing their unique value to a worldwide clientele eager to take advantage of their expertise.

With high availability of applicable knowledge and construction logic provided by web services authored by both AEC professionals and commercial software companies, the next design systems will be assembled and enhanced by and for each building project. Taking advantage of captured design intent through the mediums of building function designations, geometric representations, space planning tables and diagrams, performance requirements and regulatory constraints, future designers will orchestrate the application of scalable computation to design problems even as they orchestrate teams of experts today. They will employ these new, tireless collaborative additions to their teams to expand the scope and understanding of possible design solutions. Building proposals will be rooted in demonstrable logic and clear analyses, resulting in improved and repeatable outcomes for design firms and their clients. ◠

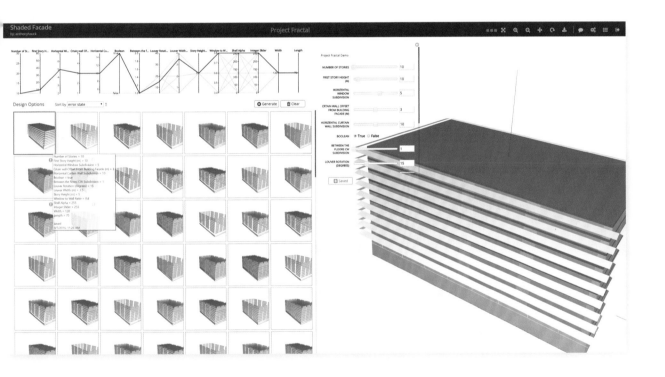

Autodesk, Facade studies, Project Fractal, 2016

This facade configuration graph uploaded to Autodesk's Project Fractal from Dynamo Studio computes and displays multiple options for fenestration distribution and shading. Characteristics of each proposal are available for display and review by the designer.

Combining Computer-Aided Geometry Design and Building Information Modelling

Shajay Bhooshan

The spatial expression and ordering of social processes is one of the primary aims of architecture. Such is the view of Zaha Hadid Architects (ZHA), where **Shajay Bhooshan** heads the computation and design group (CoDe). Here he explains how the practice has followed in the footsteps of the automotive, aircraft and shipbuilding industries in adopting a hybrid approach to design development. As demonstrated by a mathematics-themed gallery conceived by ZHA for London's Science Museum, it assimilates historical knowledge while facilitating fabrication and allowing for future flexibility.

Collaborative Design

Zaha Hadid Architects Computation and Design Group (ZHA CoDe), Typical building information modelling workflow, 2012

Through Rhino-Revit workflows, ZHA has increasingly incorporated BIM into its building design and delivery process. Through this workflow, complex geometric surfaces are mated to industry standard components such as column and glazing systems.

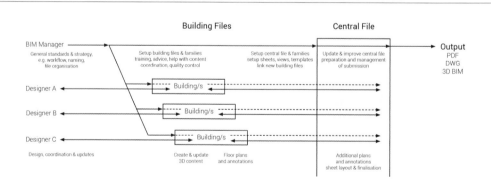

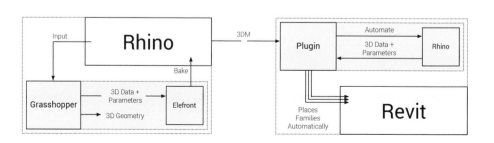

The end is to build well. Well building hath three conditions: firmness, commodity, and delight.
— Henry Wotton, 1624[1]

The purpose of architecture is often discussed in relation to Vitruvian principles of 'firmness', 'delight' and 'commodity' (as paraphrased in English by Sir Henry Wotton). Firmness – structural, environmental and technological performance of a building – and delight – spatial and formal capacities of architecture to surprise and inspire awe – are often agreed upon without much contention. Commodity – the utility or purpose of a building – however, is contended as much today as in antiquity. On the one hand, the purpose of building is often subsumed as a vehicle for technological progress. On the other, the social purpose of architecture, and architects, stakes its claims equally periodically.[2] Such disagreements on the purpose of architecture can be traced back to at least Filippo Brunelleschi and Leon Battista Alberti, famous architectural protagonists of the Italian Renaissance.[3] Recent claims of the social purpose of architecture range from the deterministic[4] – where spatial design determines the behaviour of people – to the call for its scientific study.[5]

The Purpose of Architecture

The work of Zaha Hadid Architects (ZHA) is widely recognised for its spatial and formal innovation as much as pushing engineering boundaries. It might come as a surprise to many, therefore, that the company's driving view of the ultimate purpose of architecture is aligned with that of Hillier and Hanson: architecture as the organisation of spaces and the relations of people who navigate within and occupy them.[6] Specifically, ZHA endeavours to extend Hillier's organisational science (of configuration) to include 'articulation'; that is, to make physically legible the social logic of space.[7] Thus the extended purpose of architecture becomes the augmentation of the ability of people to use spaces effectively, and the core competence of architecture becomes the ordering of social processes.[8] That this architectural ordering is best achieved by historical assimilation and collaboration between disciplines is perhaps aptly highlighted by two recent articles, 'The Congeniality of Architecture and Engineering'[9] and 'Parametricism's Structural Congeniality'.[10]

ZHA's Computation and Design Group (CoDe), initiated in 2007, has an explicit aim to align computational design with these societal purposes. Particularly, CoDe develops (early) design methods to enable an exploration of the 'organisation' and 'articulation' of space, within the bounds of physical, economic and ergonomic feasibility.

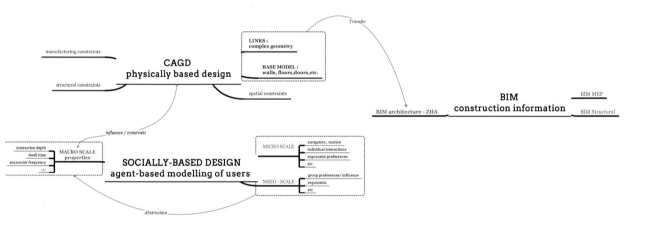

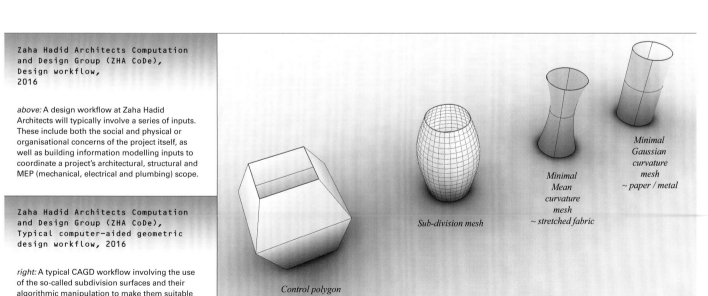

Zaha Hadid Architects Computation and Design Group (ZHA CoDe), Design workflow, 2016

above: A design workflow at Zaha Hadid Architects will typically involve a series of inputs. These include both the social and physical or organisational concerns of the project itself, as well as building information modelling inputs to coordinate a project's architectural, structural and MEP (mechanical, electrical and plumbing) scope.

Zaha Hadid Architects Computation and Design Group (ZHA CoDe), Typical computer-aided geometric design workflow, 2016

right: A typical CAGD workflow involving the use of the so-called subdivision surfaces and their algorithmic manipulation to make them suitable for fabrication.

Workflows

Associated to the purpose of building is the notion of 'workflows'. Workflows constitute the protocols of the exchange of intentions and information between clients, architects, engineers, contractors and, eventually, the users of a building. The aim of a workflow is, ultimately, to build well, i.e. to service the user. Admittedly, research efforts in the past decade have focused on computational geometry as the mediating device between architectural, engineering and manufacturing logics. The exploration of the societal purpose has, until recently, been left to accrued intuition: an intuition, to paraphrase Hillier and Hanson, to reproduce social circumstances in architectural form. Nonetheless, these efforts must be viewed in relation to the intention – as described above – eventually to subject this intuition to rational enquiry.

Workflows in design can be characterised into two paradigms – one drawing-based and the other model-based. Both drawings and models encode 2D and 3D geometry. A model, however, contains meta-information about the encoded geometry – its material specification, role in and processes of assembly, etc. On the other hand, the drawing paradigm, especially computer-aided geometric design (CAGD), can support the creation of a wider range of (arbitrarily) complex geometries, and its processing for computer-aided manufacturing (CAM). The efforts at CoDe, then, have primarily focused on developing structural- and fabrication-related meta-information for such complex geometries – in other words, augmenting complex CAGD objects with construction-specific information. Such hybrid approaches capture the best of both worlds and allow the, thus far intuitive, exploration of organisation and articulation.

Zaha Hadid Architects Computation and Design Group (ZHA CoDe),
Volu Dining Pavilion,
Miami,
2015

For the Volu Dining Pavilion in Miami, the computer-aided geometric design (CAGD) workflow involved the analysis of various configurations of the structural shell, a rationalisation of the manufacturing process, and the algorithmic generation of shell componentry for machine production. The project, which occupied about 20 square metres (215 square feet), was one of a series of prefabricated living spaces initiated by Revolution, a project by Miami real estate developer Robbie Antonio.

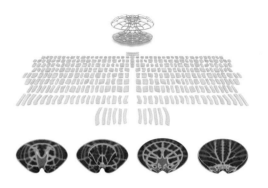

Algorithmic processing of CAGD geometries to ensure suitability for fabrication.

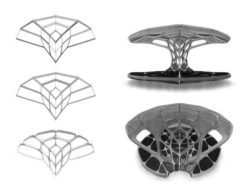

The finished and installed Volu Dining Pavilion.

Workflows in CAGD

The ubiquitous drawing-based paradigm, popularly known as computer-aided drafting (CAD), is widely acknowledged to have started with the invention of Sketchpad at MIT.[11] The automotive, aircraft and shipbuilding industries were among the earliest to develop this paradigm to include capabilities of mathematically describing complex surfaces (CAGD) and computer-controlled manufacture (CAM). An essential aspect of such CAGD environments is the abstraction of complex physical phenomena and machine parameters associated with the manufacturing method into geometric properties and constraints – something famously demonstrated by Ivan Sutherland in his 1963 Sketchpad prototype software. Seminal examples include the development and use of Bézier curves and surfaces,[12] physical splines, 'developable' surfaces, etc. Additionally, in these industries, singular corporations such as Boeing or Citroën own the entire design, production and assembly pipeline. Thus, collaboration between design, engineering and manufacturing disciplines is usually more comprehensive and internal to the large corporation and characterised by predominantly encapsulated, linear and non-iterative workflows.

Such encapsulated workflows have a pre-computer history in architectural design. Andrew Witt eloquently traces the use of geometric methods in architectural and structural design since the Renaissance.[13] Further, he indicates the usefulness of such methods in the abstraction of mathematical knowledge into drawing instruments for specific types of complex geometry, and manuals of construction for their physical realisation in materials such as stone and timber. This led to a profusion of innovation and widespread assimilation of the material and construction technology within the building economy, i.e. geometric 'design explorers'[14] of the period not only embedded the structural stability of the design but also guaranteed its construction feasibility, thus contributing to its assimilation.

More recently Frank Gehry, whose architecture is known for its use of developable surfaces, initiated the development of the Digital Project software platform to enable the design and construction of his projects. Recent developments in the field of architectural geometry, with its explicit aim of 'incorporation of essential aspects of function, fabrication and statics into the shape modelling process',[15] extend this CAGD paradigm to contemporary architectural design.

Workflows in BIM

Building information modelling (BIM), a data-driven model-based workflow, has almost the same extent of history as CAGD. The model-based paradigm, leading to current-day BIM, had a quieter inception in 1975 with a visionary paper by Charles Eastman, 'The Use of Computers Instead of Drawings in Building Design'.[16] BIM, since its inception, is specifically tailored to the building industry. It is arguably also more amenable to the collaborative and iterative workflows of the architecture, engineering and construction (AEC) industry. This collaborative workflow is historically necessitated. A brief summary of the evolution of the relationships between the primary stakeholders – clients, architects, engineers, contractors – reveals this.

Andrew Saint notes that, during the last century, engineers have variably been consultants to architects and their contracting engineers, and also held the rarefied status of specialist problem-solving engineers for complex geometries.[17] This increasing specialisation and distinction has been attributed as much to the advent of new materials and rational design,[18] as to the ascendancy of new applied science and mathematics.[19] Similarly, the role differentiation and specialisation of the building contractor have been attributed both to the business acumen of entrepreneurs like François Hennebique[20] and the boom of new building types such as the skyscraper and its attendant economic pressures, the need for sophisticated building trades, technologies such as elevators, supply chains and management.[21] Lastly, the relationship between the architect and end-user has also changed dramatically – prior to the First World War, end-users of buildings were the dominant clientele of an architect. Post-war building booms meant that the distance – both in terms of social class and administration – between the user and the architect grew and there was little or no direct relationship.[22]

Hybrid Workflows

ZHA has adopted a hybrid approach between the two paradigms – the abstracted, encapsulated paradigm of CAGD and CAM and the collaborative, project-specific workflows of BIM. For instance, a typical workflow begins with the use of a widely employed geometric description from the computer graphics industry – the so-called 'subdivision surfaces'. CoDe has investigated the benefits of this geometric description in architectural design.[23] It has also attempted to turn this into a CAGD object via its combination with numerical modelling techniques to abstract its physical realisation with fabric,[24] curved-crease folded metal[25] and 3D printing.[26] Variations of this workflow have been employed in large-scale projects in collaborations with engineers. ZHA's Mathematics: The Winton Gallery at the Science Museum in London (2016) illustrates the benefits of such a workflow – its capacity to assimilate historic knowledge, enabling of collaboration and iteration, amenability to digital fabrication, etc.

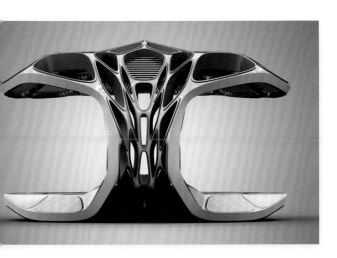

Computer-generated elevational view of the pavilion.

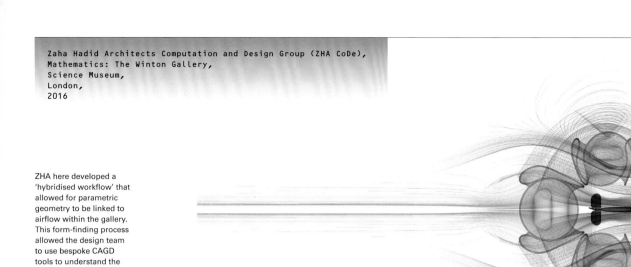

ZHA here developed a 'hybridised workflow' that allowed for parametric geometry to be linked to airflow within the gallery. This form-finding process allowed the design team to use bespoke CAGD tools to understand the gallery both spatially and structurally. BIM was used to parametrically develop 91 display cases and the display of 130 individual objects in the gallery.

Data-driven layouts: bespoke tools were developed to manage constantly changing and refining object lists, curatorial narratives and the subsequent spatial layout of the objects that satisfied various ergonomic, experiential and spatial requirements.

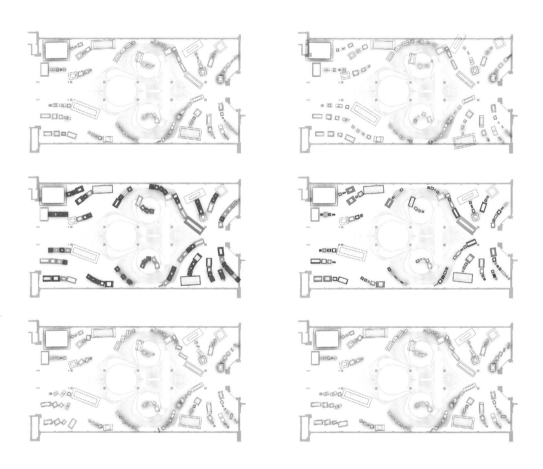

Name	Index	Zone	Story	Casing ID	PlinthType	Object Type	Interpretation	Interpretation2	OpeningType	OpeningTypePlinth	SilicaType	CasingType	Date	ObjectZ	Object X	ObjectY
Hadley Page Aeroplane	1	0	1	_	0	1	1	0	0	0	0	1	1929	2780	11860	7880
Castlereagh Collection (2 Boxes)	2	1	2	1	3	2	_	0	4	0	0	3	1815	2050	1320	370
Bronze Exchequer Gallon Measure	3	1	2	2	3	3	_	0	3	2	0	3	1601	254	230	190
Bronze Exchequer Quart Measure	4	1	2	2	3	3	_	0	3	2	0	3	1601	133	170	135
Bronze Exchequer Pint Measure	5	1	2	2	3	3	_	0	3	2	0	3	1601	108	135	108
Queen Elizabeth Exchequer Avoirdupois weights	6	1	2	2	3	3	_	0	3	2	0	3	1588	90	150	150
Elizabeth exchequer End standard yard	7	1	2	2	3	3	_	0	3	2	0	3	1588	18	910	14
Bronze mural tablet with standard measures	8	1	2	_	1	3	_	0	0	0	0	1	1893	500	1235	75
Set of 8 brass handled inspectors imperial weights	9	1	2	3	3	3	8	0	1	2	0	2	1890	330	380	350

Mathematics: The Winton Gallery, Science Museum, London

The computational methods employed to generate the shapes and spaces of the gallery were a result of a fluid exchange of means, methods and models across disciplines. For instance, the simulation of the airflow around the key figuring object of the Handley Page aeroplane has a lineage in the physics of fluid dynamics dating back to Claude-Louis Navier and George Gabriel Stokes in the 19th century. Further, they were made accessible and amenable for use in early, interactive stages of design by sustained research in computational fluid dynamics by the likes of Jos Stam[27] and others from the computer animation industry. Thus, ZHA was able to utilise the actual models and code as opposed to merely drawing inspiration from the formal appearance of fluid-flows. Such interdisciplinary osmosis in the early stages transmuted into more clearly defined roles for architects, engineers and contractors in the later stages of the project. Simple yet bespoke building information modelling enabled a well-coordinated execution of the project.

Central to any gallery are the curatorial vision and the objects themselves. It is therefore natural to make the objects and the narrative the motivating driver for the spatial organisation of the gallery. Additionally, if the objects change, the spatial organisation has to accommodate this change. The approach to this was a data-driven one. The first step was to tabulate the data of the hundred-odd objects, their 91 display cases and their relation to their principal storyline and also the remaining 25 storylines, their position within 6 categories, dimensional information, sensitivity to light, requirements of preservation, etc. A bespoke algorithm then processed the information and laid out the objects to negotiate the often disparate requirements – curatorial vision, object dimensions, ease of navigation, available space, access and circulation requirements, and construction costs. This enabled the spatial layout of the gallery to be changed easily were the objects, stories or any another aspect of the curatorial vision to change.

Primary user navigation and storyline distribution are naturally emphasised using spatial and easy-to-register aspects such as curvature, fluid and interrupted visual field, etc. This is further accentuated by resonance in several other ancillary features such as the lighting and floor-tile layout, colour scheme, height distribution of the display cases, etc. All the major features of the space thus become inter-correlated and cohesive with the human navigation and occupation of the spaces.

The geometry and materialisation of these central organising features of the gallery are a result of both a practical transfer of knowledge across disciplines and a lineage of fabric structures that the office has undertaken in the past. The geometry of these constructs – so-called minimal surfaces – was intensively studied by pioneering architect-engineer Frei Otto. These geometries have also been studied mathematically.[28] Their computational 'generation' – a so-called form-finding process – usually employs one of two popular methods – the dynamic relaxation method and the force density method. These seminal methods have been made more accessible to architects and engineers alike by research institutions like the Block Research Group[29] and the University of Bath.[30]

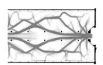

above: Predicted user analytics: bespoke tools were developed to understand the experiential aspects of a typical visitor – overall visibility, plausible dwell routes, hard and soft obstacles, etc. Such visualisations had to be carried out each time the gallery layout and geometry changed.

left: View of the completed gallery.

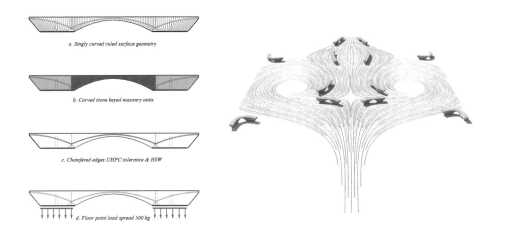

a. Singly curved ruled surface geometry

b. Carved stone keyed masonry units

c. Chamfered edges: UHPC tolerance & HSW

d. Floor point load spread 500 kg

top and centre: Significant to the visitor experience in the Mathematics gallery design was the form and location of bench seating. Benches were originally formed through the extraction of curve geometry from the fluid lines and then developed first as ruled surfaces and then as solid objects, which could be fabricated via robotic hot-wire-cutting of moulds.

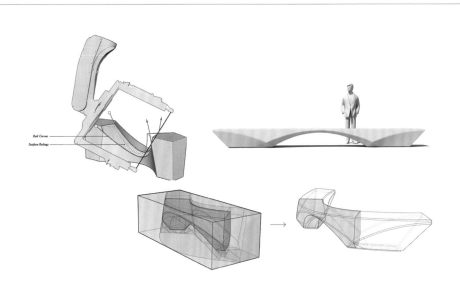

The gallery was populated by a series of 'fabric pods' that were controlled by edge curves imagined as bent pipes. Analyses built into the CAGD workflow ensured these pipes could be bent to achieve the geometric curvature imagined by the design team. This process was ultimately tested through a series of physical models.

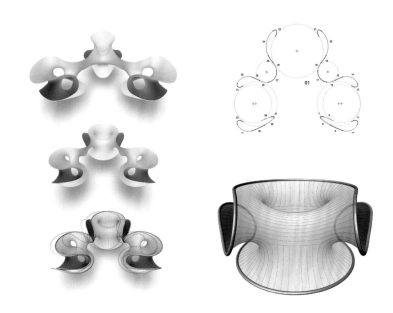

The gallery has several moments of 'pause' including 14 benches – designed as cast, ultra-high-performance concrete benches. The shape and physical production of this furniture also owe their development to a long lineage of research into the mathematics, engineering and materialisation of a certain class of surfaces called 'ruled surfaces'. Mathematically these surfaces have been known for centuries, but in-depth study of them gained traction after the invention of calculus and is widely credited to French mathematician Gaspard Monge.[31] These surfaces were very prominent and widely used in 19th-century masonry and timber structures. The benches of the gallery inherit this mathematical, physical and material history and employ it in a contemporary setting. This involved collaboration with a state-of-the-art robotic company specialising in the hot-wire cutting of foam to produce the moulds for the cast concrete.

A Renewed Focus

The design of bespoke workflows for building projects is motivated by the desire to build well, novel computational technologies, and the evolving complexity of relations between architects, engineers and contractors. These parameters also necessitate that workflows combine the benefits of both drawing-based and model-based paradigms of computational design. Arguably, this hybrid approach has been preoccupied by formal and performance aspects of buildings. This preoccupation, however, has exposed a vast solution space of economically and ergonomically feasible possibilities. These possibilities enable a systemic focus of computational design on the ultimate purpose of architecture – a social purpose of space. A purpose hitherto left to intuition. ⌂

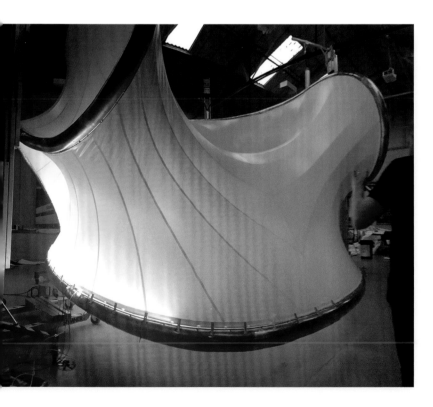

Prototype of the 'fabric pod'.

Notes
1. Henry Wotton, *The Elements of Architecture*, John Bill (London), 1624, p 1.
2. Alan Lipman, 'The Architectural Belief System and Social Behaviour', *British Journal of Sociology*, 20 (2), June 1969, pp 190–204.
3. Andrew J Witt, 'A Machine Epistemology in Architecture: Encapsulated Knowledge and the Instrumentation of Design', *Candide: Journal for Architectural Knowledge*, 3 (3), 2010, pp 37–88.
4. Maurice Broady, 'Social Theory in Architectural Design', in Robert Gutman (ed), *People and Buildings*, Basic Books (New York), 1972.
5. Bill Hillier and Julienne Hanson, *The Social Logic of Space*, Cambridge University Press (Cambridge, MA), 1989.
6. *Ibid*.
7. Patrik Schumacher, 'Tectonic Articulation: Making Engineering Logics Speak', in Mark Garcia (ed), *Δ Future Details of Architecture*, July/August 2014 (no 4), pp 44–51.
8. Patrik Schumacher, 'Design Parameters to Parametric Design', in Mitra Kanaani and Dak Kopec (eds), *The Routledge Companion for Architecture Design and Practice: Established and Emerging Trends*, Routledge (New York), 2014.
9. Patrik Schumacher, 'The Congeniality of Architecture and Engineering', in Sigrid Adriaenssens et al (eds), *Shell Structures for Architecture: Form Finding and Optimization*, Routledge (New York), 2014, p 271.
10. Philippe Block, 'Parametricism's Structural Congeniality', in Patrik Schumacher (ed), *Δ Parameticism 2.0: Rethinking Parameticism for the 21st Century*, March/April 2016 (no 2), pp 68–75.
11. Ivan E Sutherland, 'Sketchpad: A Man-Machine Graphical Communication System', in *Proceedings of the SHARE Design Automation Workshop*, ACM (New York), 1964, pp 6.329–46.
12. Pierre E Bézier, 'Example of an Existing System in the Motor Industry: The Unisurf System', in *Proceedings of the Royal Society of London A: Mathematical, Physical and Engineering Sciences*, The Royal Society (London), 321 (1545), 1971, pp 207–18.
13. Witt, *op cit*.
14. Axel Kilian, 'Design Exploration through Bidirectional Modeling of Constraints', unpublished PhD thesis, Massachusetts Institute of Technology (Cambridge, MA), 2006.
15. Caigui Jiang et al, 'Interactive Modeling of Architectural Freeform Structures: Combining Geometry with Fabrication and Statics', in Philippe Bock et al (eds), *Advances in Architectural Geometry 2014*, Springer (Cham), 2015, pp 95–108.
16. Charles M Eastman, 'The Use of Computers Instead of Drawings in Building Design', *AIA Journal*, 63 (3), 1975, pp 46–50.
17. Andrew Saint, *Architect and Engineer: A Study in Sibling Rivalry*, Yale University Press (New Haven, CT, and London), 2007.
18. Hans Straub, *A History of Civil Engineering: An Outline from Ancient to Modern Times*, L Hill (London), 1964.
19. Antoine Picon, 'Navier and the Introduction of Suspension Bridges in France', *Construction History*, 4, 1988, pp 21–34.
20. Patricia Cusack, 'Agents of Change: Hennebique, Mouchel and Ferroconcrete in Britain, 1897–1908', *Construction History*, 3, 1987, pp 61–74.
21. Jane Bonshek, 'The Skyscraper: A Catalyst of Change in the Chicago Construction Industries, 1882–1892', *Construction History*, 4, 1988, pp 53–74.
22. Lipman, *op cit*.
23. Shajay Bhooshan and Mostafa El Sayed, 'Use of Sub-Division Surfaces in Architectural Form-Finding and Procedural Modelling', in *Proceedings of the International Conference on Simulation for Architecture and Urbanism*, Society for Computer Simulation International (San Diego, CA), 2011, pp 60–67.
24. Shajay Bhooshan and Mostafa El Sayed, 'Sub-Division Surfaces in Architectural Form Finding and Fabric Forming', in *Proceedings of the Second International Conference on Flexible Formwork*, University of Bath (Bath), 2012, pp 64–74.
25. Shajay Bhooshan, 'Interactive Design of Curved Crease Folding', unpublished PhD thesis, University of Bath (Bath), 2016.
26. Shajay Bhooshan, 'Upgrading Computational Design', in Patrik Schumacher (ed), *Δ Parameticism 2.0: Rethinking Parameticism for the 21st Century*, March/April 2016 (no 2), pp 44–53.
27. Jos Stam, 'Real-Time Fluid Dynamics for Games', in *Proceedings of the Game Developer Conference*, UBM (London), 2003, p 25.
28. Kenneth A Brakke, 'Minimal Surfaces, Corners, and Wires', *Journal of Geometric Analysis*, 2 (1), 1992, pp 11–36.
29. Sigrid Adriaenssens et al (eds), *Shell Structures for Architecture: Form Finding and Optimization*, Routledge (New York), 2014.
30. CJK Williams, 'Defining and Designing Curved Flexible Tensile Surface Structures', in JA Gregory (ed), *The Mathematics of Surfaces*, Clarendon (Oxford), 1986, pp 143–77.
31. Snežana Lawrence, 'Developable Surfaces: Their History and Application', *Nexus Network Journal*, 13 (3), 2011, pp 701–14.

Ruptured

Kutan Ayata

An Argument for Nonlinear Workflows

Does the quest for efficiency in design-to-fabrication software risk producing a sterile, homogenised built environment? Not if architects are prepared to disrupt digital workflows at key stages, spurring alternative aesthetics. New York practice Young & Ayata have a particular interest in the opportunities for reinterpretation and redirection that are opened up by moments of transition between mediums. **Kutan Ayata**, one of the firm's founding partners, outlines their approach, illustrating it through two projects on vastly differing scales where they have sought to exploit these shifts.

Young & Ayata,
*Still Life with Lemon,
Goblet and Geological Rub
Object after Willem Claesz,
1646–2014*

The realism of the Donkeys and Feathers vessel as a thing in the world is further explored through a project in rendering and photocomposition, whereby it is inserted into a 17th-century Dutch still life painting. The object is adjusted through rendering and composition to address the issues of colour, light, texture and reflection to heighten the plausibility of the painting's realism.

Flows

Evaluating the legitimacy and success of an architectural proposal by the rigour of its process is a well-established approach in the discipline. This is either through the means of its fabrication or construction, or through the processes that constitute the emergence and development of its design. While the former celebrates building technologies, techniques and materials in the realm of physical construction, the latter generally navigates various modes of design, production and representational mediums to stake a position in the theoretical trajectories of architecture. This second method of evaluation is common within the academic environment where students are asked to demonstrate a meaningful series of related design acts to justify a proposal, as though the real qualities and potential consequences of an architectural project can only be verified through a logical chain of events and set of relatable abstract constructs generated during its inception.

Young & Ayata,
Geological Vessel,
Donkeys and Feathers,
2014

Rasterised version of a vector field drawing that depicts normals and tangents to a set of base curves. The absence of the original curves and the dense frequency of normals and tangents begin to render a surface with a particular material character.

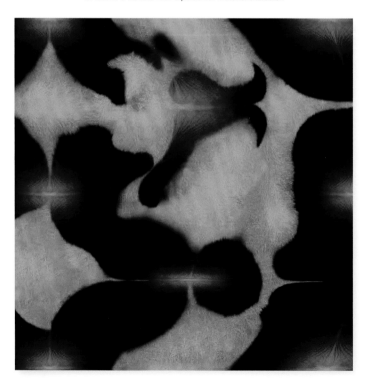

Serial Workflows: Form Follows Arrow/Data

The advancement of digital technology has accelerated the evaluation of architecture through process in two prominent directions. Although the aesthetic outcomes are different, both are typically organised as serial workflows. In the first one, the process of form making is reduced to an overly simplified step-by-step diagram aspiring to communicate to a broader audience in the name of public inclusion; this requires a recipe-like execution to help 'make sense' of the formal transformations, aka 'form follows arrow'. All complexities of architecture are reduced to consumable graphics. In the second, an overly redundant set of steps regarding the generation of form is displayed to demonstrate various software protocols, parameter performance, data inclusion and stages of digital maturation. Again, this is a serial workflow documenting justifiable evidence of formal becoming, aka 'form follows data'. All complexities of architecture are reduced to technological input and variation.

Graphical or technological, both processes ultimately result in justifying the architectural aesthetic through the logic of process. Here, we will not further debate the problems of projects foregrounding process as their central locus, but rather touch upon the aesthetic potential of rupturing or estranging the logic of workflows. This is an effort to question procedural grounding, knowable essence and an ideal aesthetics of the eventual architectural object. But, of course, to rupture process still requires one.

The reality is that architecture is not a medium-specific effort. Drawings, renderings, models, prototypes, scripts, simulations, texts, lectures and buildings are all put forward by architects. The multiplicity of mediums through which architects navigate to set forth ideas and implement material manifestations presents challenges as well as potentials. At Young & Ayata, a New York-based architectural practice, interest lies in the moments of transition across mediums where (mis)translations, accidents, glitches, limits, interpretations and re-appropriations might suggest unexpected aesthetic provocations. Following are two projects through which Young & Ayata have attempted to exploit these shifts between various mediums.

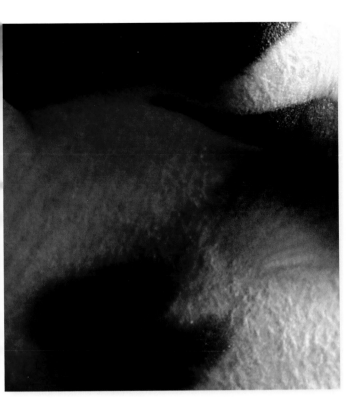

Close-up detail of surface articulation shows the erasure of any traces of the underlying geometric substructure of the mapped image as well as any residue of the powder as the material of construction. The surface acquires a soft, almost a suede-like visual quality, which proves otherwise through the feel of the plasticised powder upon contact.

The 3D (powder) printed object is articulated with the mapped image on its surface. At times, the various axes of local asymmetries on the mapped image tactically match the cusp line of the vessel and perform ornamentally to heighten the object's form. When there is misalignment between the cusp and the axis in the image, the patterning begins to behave more decoratively, heightening the surface quality.

Donkeys and Feathers

This project is the design and fabrication of four objects with distinctly different aesthetic qualities, which are achieved through varied surface articulations in texture, colour and finish. Each object in this series was conceived through the grafting of a drawing on to a simple vessel-like form, which was then 3D (powder) printed. The drawings are autonomous pieces realised independently from this design exercise. The drawing technique used for these representations is built from straight lines, tangents and normals to a series of interpolated curves, adjusted according to various criteria of rate of change in curvature, colour, density and depth. These drawings have symmetrical organisations that are then exploited in their application to the object's surfaces.

The vessel-like form is a rather simple volume that is cusped into creases at two points to deny the reduction of its figure to a single contour. The cusps also define two distinctly different profiles for the object. The axis of the grafted drawing at times tactically matches the cusp line and performs ornamentally to heighten the object's form. When there is misalignment between the cusp and the axis of the drawing, the patterning begins to behave more decoratively and heightens the surface quality. The grafted volume then receives various articulations in its mesh count and surface relief to produce a range of aesthetic qualities. The aesthetic play here is one of doubt between the optical and tactile where the digitally fabricated object shifts the association of its medium (powder) and gains characteristics of another material. The result is that these implied material associations give them a strange reality.

Each object in this series was conceived through the grafting of a drawing on to a simple vessel-like form, which was then 3D (powder) printed.

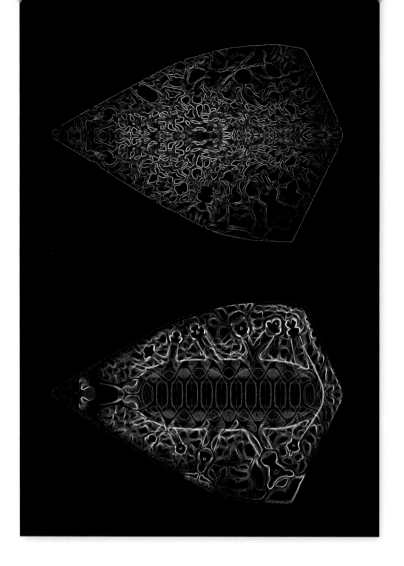

Dalseong Citizen's Gymnasium

This is a competition proposal for a public gymnasium situated on hilly terrain in Dalseong, South Korea. The project questions the site through an aesthetic estrangement of the ground. The base of this ground as a plan view is established with the manipulation of a found image that inherently had qualities of non-linear organisation, varied subdivision and a deep surface relief. The image was accepted for what it is and appropriated according to the demands and criteria of the architectural project, which is to be buried beneath the surface of a mound.

The image was subject to cropping to define the site's range and scale, global mirroring to establish axial symmetry, and strategic mirroring for local symmetries to loosely organise the territory. Through the mediation of a contour drawing based on the height-field surface model of the image, a transition from pixel to surface to vector, the site appears to curdle into a molten mess. What was so far a rather generic and procedural set of operations was followed by surgical and local crafting of the building geometry into the complex field lines of the terrain contours. This manual drawing operation helped fully integrate the autonomous entities of the ground and the buried building into a cohesive whole. The strangeness of this aesthetic decision could best be observed in an X-ray plan drawing.

above top: Contour lines extracted from the digital height-field surface, the result of a process that transitions the design from pixel to surface and finally into the vector domain of line drawing.

above bottom: X-ray plan highlighting the crafted integration between the contour lines of the landscape and the building geometry, both of which are constructs of unrelated criteria and origin.

Young & Ayata,
Dalseong Citizen's Gymnasium,
Dalseong,
South Korea,
2014

In this competition proposal, the source image of a (random) material behaviour is mirrored to establish the main axis of symmetry for the project. Dark, symmetrical figures have been inserted in a painterly fashion to distort the initial global symmetry.

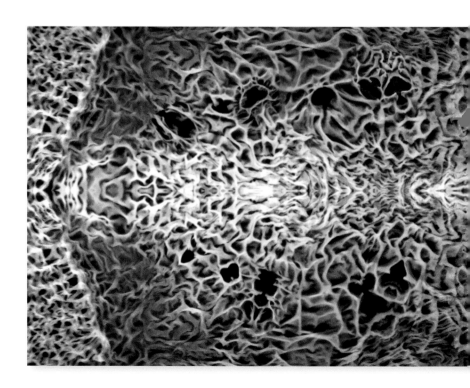

A Matter of Subjectivity

The starting points for both projects are very similar in that they both commence utilising images with organisations of symmetry, field complexity and local figuration. While one of them is an artificial and abstract construction of geometric definition (tangents and normals), the other one is a photographic image of a material behaviour. It should be clear that the inherent content of these images bears little significance in the production, consequence and aesthetic provocations of the final design work. What is critical in this particular approach to design is to find a way of disrupting a traditionally linear process within the context of each project as it is navigated through multiple mediums with the end goal of defining an aesthetic agenda.

For Young & Ayata, this rupture or estrangement of workflow logic produces a heightened attention to the aesthetic qualities of each stage in the process. This does not dismiss process in design, but instead focuses on the difference in each stage as an aesthetic object in its own right. It is not the logic of the system that matters, but the ruptures that challenge the design to articulate alternate aesthetics.

Pre-packaged software, bundled digital definitions, open source scripts, highly effective building information models, 3D printing technologies, robotic fabrication protocols and many other digital design/output interfaces are at the architect's disposal. All of them are powerful mediums through which to speculate on the future of the built environment. It is apparent that the potential for pure efficiency in these interfaces, pressured by the forces of capitalism, will result in homogenised outcomes. At this juncture, the critical issue is the subjective manner in which the architectural profession engages these protocols to plot a different and perhaps stranger version of that future. ⅅ

Aerial view of the final proposal showing the fully integrated architectural object in its 'new' ground.

For Young & Ayata, this rupture or estrangement of workflow logic produces a heightened attention to the aesthetic qualities of each stage in the process.

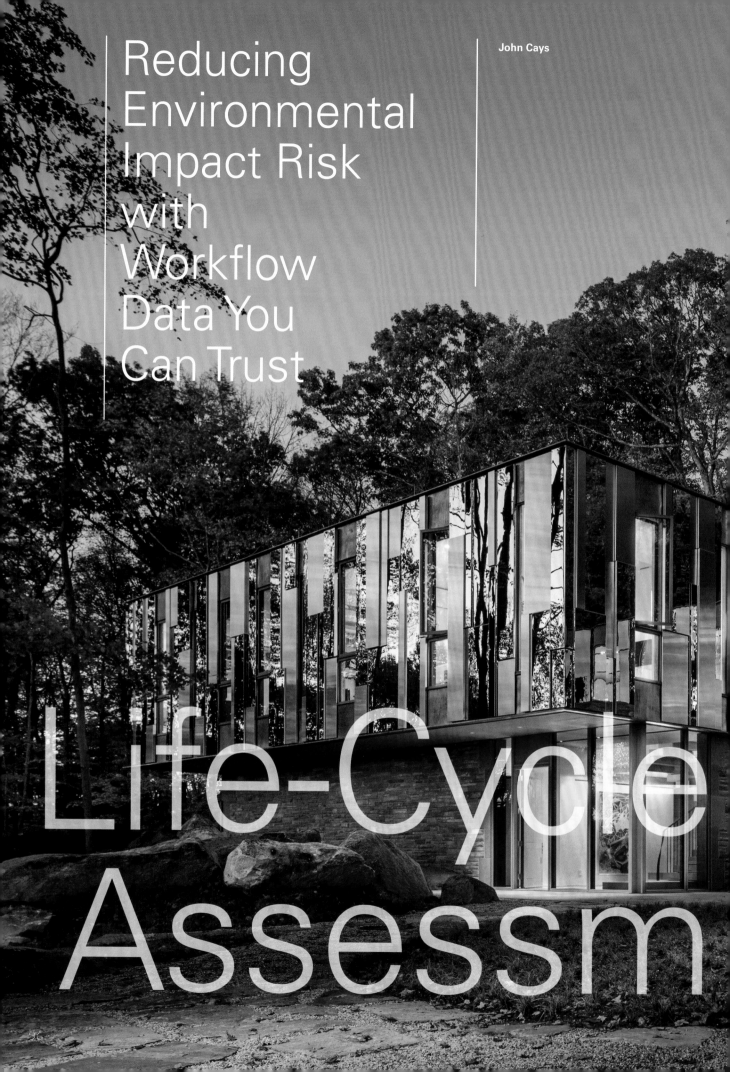

Reducing
Environmental
Impact Risk
with
Workflow
Data You
Can Trust

John Cays

Life-Cycle
Assessm

How can architects offer proof of their proposals' 'green' credentials? The answer – as advocated by **John Cays**, Associate Dean of the New Jersey Institute of Technology's College of Architecture and Design – is through life-cycle assessment (LCA). Here he explains what it is, tracing its evolution over some six decades. He goes on to describe how design firms are partnering with software developers to create LCA tools that work alongside building information modelling to generate reliable data on their projects' ecological profiles.

ent

KieranTimberlake,
Pound Ridge House,
Pound Ridge,
New York,
2014

KieranTimberlake here used Tally to evaluate the environmental impacts of a residential project. Careful impact analysis of each constituent element in a design does not necessarily limit the creative use of materials, as evidenced here in the expressive use and composition of durable exterior finishes: zinc-coated copper, brushed stainless steel, polished stainless steel and glass.

KieranTimberlake here used Tally to evaluate the environmental impacts of a residential project. Careful impact analysis of each constituent element in a design does not necessarily limit the creative use of materials, as evidenced here in the expressive use and composition of durable exterior finishes:

Rapidly evolving life-cycle assessment (LCA) methods and tools provide data-driven insight into how the human proclivity to do and make things, in ever increasing quantities, impacts the planet. LCA improves how people observe, measure and display the effects of our individual and cumulative daily actions. This is key to changing our practices and behaviours for the better.

Architects and designers work at the beginning of this process. The decisions they make set the trajectory for good or ill. In order to satisfy the demand for 'green design', they regularly make claims regarding sustainability. Their claims, however, are rarely supported by verifiable data. Design professionals can move beyond reductionist, point-based checklist approaches to make and support design decisions that can oversimplify inherently complex problems. Architects can benefit from emerging tools that directly integrate trustworthy LCA methods and data into their design workflows.

As the incorporation of environmental data into these workflows becomes ever more automatic, seamless and painless, architects can provide more and better services to the design market. Clients increasingly want to know how their building will perform across a number of metrics, including how it will impact the environment. LCA tools, recently developed for architects, coupled with increasing LCA data quantity and quality can help satisfy this demand. Architects therefore need to be encouraged to take advantage of this emerging approach to provide clients with better answers.

What is LCA and Why Should We Use it?

Ideally, an LCA produces a comprehensive and neutral technical document. It compiles and presents copious, detailed and accurate data on inputs and outputs – what gets taken from and given back to the earth – throughout each stage of a product

or service life cycle, along with a projection of its potential impact on the environment and human health. It tells the quantitative story of each raw material extracted from the earth and the energy required to process, deliver and maintain it as a finished product or service, as well as what is left to deal with after it no longer serves its main purpose at the conclusion of its life cycle.

LCA is fundamentally abstract and technical, as opposed to visual and intuitive, which may account for its slow adoption by most architecture firms. However, currently available evolving tools that work with architects' BIM workflows, such as KieranTimberlake's Tally, can take the detailed accounting drudgery out of the workflow, and will help more architects integrate LCA into their design practices.

Life-cycle phase definitions and cost analyses have their roots in the 1950s. Developed by the economist David Novick while working for the RAND Corporation, they were originally used

KieranTimberlake, Diagram contrasting traditional and Tally workflows, 2015

KieranTimberlake's Tally integrates LCA data into the design workflow with an ease and speed that promotes iterative decision making so that designers can work to reduce environmental impact over the course of the entire design process.

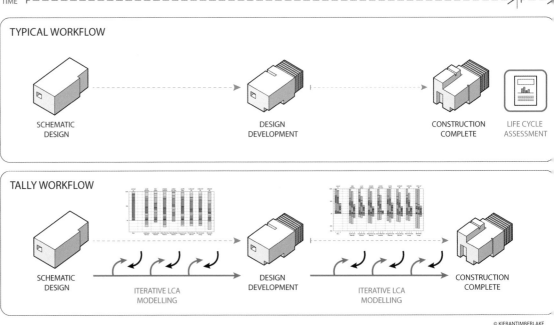

© KIERANTIMBERLAKE

LCA is fundamentally abstract and technical, as opposed to visual and intuitive, which may account for its slow adoption by most architecture firms.

KieranTimberlake,
Brown University School
of Engineering,
Providence,
Rhode Island,
due for completion 2018

Life-cycle assessment (LCA)
methods guided the design
decisions at Brown University's
School of Engineering.
KieranTimberlake's research
division continues to develop
new techniques and tools, like
their Tally software, to help make
LCA data relevant to architects
inhouse and to the wider
architectural profession.

tally

Structural System Options
- Option 1 - Concrete
- Option 2 - Steel (primary)
- Option 3 - Steel (fly ash)

CSI Divisions
- 03 - Concrete
- 05 - Metals
- 06 - Wood/Plastics/Composites
- 07 - Thermal and Moisture Protection
- 08 - Openings and Glazing
- 09 - Finishes

Brown University School for Engineering

Tally screenshot comparing
steel and concrete structural
systems for Brown University
School of Engineering. As a
leader in the use of LCA for
buildings, KieranTimberlake's
research division developed
an in-house custom software
solution called Tally to bridge
the gap between abstract
assessment and practical
material choices on this and
many other projects.

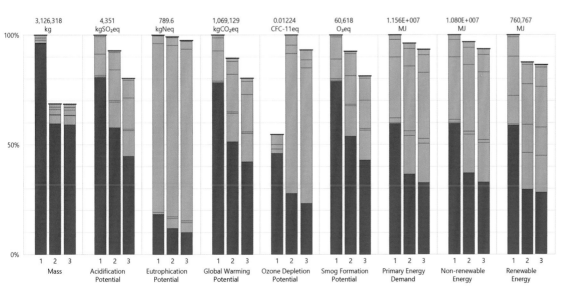

3,126,318 kg	4,351 kgSO₂eq	789.6 kgNeq	1,069,129 kgCO₂eq	0.01224 CFC-11eq	60,618 O₃eq	1.156E+007 MJ	1.080E+007 MJ	760,767 MJ

Mass | Acidification Potential | Eutrophication Potential | Global Warming Potential | Ozone Depletion Potential | Smog Formation Potential | Primary Energy Demand | Non-renewable Energy | Renewable Energy

John Cays, Life-cycle boundary
conditions, New Jersey Institute
of Technology (NJIT), Newark,
New Jersey, 2016

LCA allows architects and designers to
consider the schematic life-cycle boundary
relationships between typical building phases.
These include material production and
manufacturing, building construction, and
post-occupancy to end-of-life cycles as well
as options for reuse and recycling through
these phases.

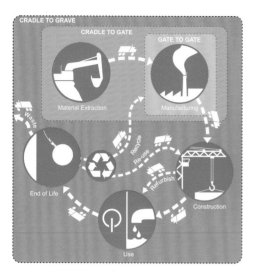

John Cays, Life-cycle assessment
framework diagram after ISO
14040, New Jersey Institute of
Technology (NJIT), Newark, New
Jersey, 2016

The different stages of an LCA (adapted from
ISO 14040). Each stage requires the assessor
to work iteratively, in order to identify the
materially important information in the study.

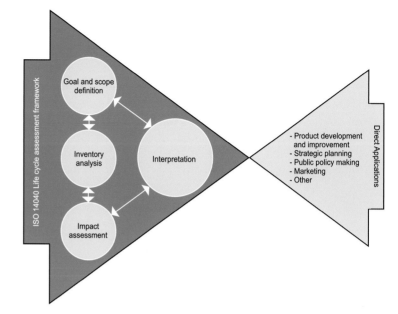

by the US military to improve budget
management of weapon systems.
They focused on costs, beginning
with research and development and
continuing through the use phase
through to final decommissioning. By
the late 1960s, private corporations
had begun to apply these concepts to
analyse solid waste production and
energy use to maximise operational
efficiency. Environmental life-cycle
assessment, as distinct from life-cycle
costing, emerged in the 1980s. Its
methods and procedures, formalised
in the 1990s, were documented in the
International Standards Organization
(ISO) 14040 series,[1] which was
updated and consolidated in 2006,
and outlines the methodological
framework, rules and regulations that
guide LCA activities today.[2]

In determining a product's
possible impact on the environment
throughout its life cycle, companies
typically measure and document
five key areas: its potential to create
acid rain (increase acidification), kill
streams, rivers and oceans (promote
eutrophication), make smog (create
tropospheric ozone), make the hole

in the ozone layer bigger (decrease
stratospheric ozone), and make the
earth warmer (produce greenhouse
gas). After assessing all available,
relevant and compliant data related
to each impact category, a numerical
total is then assigned to the product
or service.

Additional assessments, depending
on need and the method followed, can
measure the potential to deplete fossil
fuel resources, reduce the amount of
usable land available to all species,
decrease the amount of usable water,
poison the environment with toxic
chemicals (eco-toxicity), and increase
risks to human health.

LCA practitioners follow
established ISO protocols to set
boundary conditions around the most
important parts of their studies. These
can include cradle to gate, gate to gate,
and gate to grave (or cradle when
materials are repurposed or recycled).
Primary and secondary effects may
be considered, but anything beyond
these, usually influencing significantly
less than 1 per cent of the product,
is excluded. For example, the
environmental impact attributed to the

equipment used to make a truck that
delivers the steel for a building to site
would not be counted in construction-
phase evaluations.

LCA Methods and Tools

Irrespective of the operational details
that guide LCA studies, when clients
ask a question about the health
or environmental impacts of their
proposed building, they expect the
answers they receive from architects
to be supported by established,
trustworthy and transparent analysis
and reporting methods. LCA
represents a substantial improvement
over self-referential sustainable
design evaluation frameworks.
Its practitioners evaluate multiple
parameters affecting the assessment
and must exercise judgement at
numerous points along the way
throughout a highly iterative process
before a final assessment is produced.

Two distinct top-level LCA
modelling methods, attributional and
consequential, serve fundamentally
different needs. Attributional LCA
bases its conclusions on established
data about the cumulative

environmental impacts of each known linear process at work throughout a product's life cycle. Often, this type of assessment is used to support a company's published Environmental Product Declaration (EPD). EPDs have been called a product's 'nutritional label', and designers can also use individual EPDs as detailed technical cut sheets in a set of project documents. Ambitious, complex, and often controversial consequential LCA models are used primarily by policymakers to consider the implications of large-scale, linear and nonlinear systems such as the end effects of various regional and national land-use planning alternatives or consumer behaviour dynamics. The LCA tools that most directly inform architects' decisions primarily leverage the more straightforward attributional LCA level work, grounded in life-cycle inventory (LCI) data.

Both publicly available government databases and proprietary LCI databases contain specific, detailed and usable inventories of the impacts of industrial manufacturing processes. The German company thinkstep's GaBi LCA tool (GaBi is short for 'Ganzheitliche Bilanz', which is the German for 'holistic balance') provides useful portals to these growing life-cycle inventories. Top-level dashboard software directly integrates this information into design workflows without requiring users to perform separate, detailed life-cycle assessments of each material assembly or pore over individual product EPDs. Autodesk's Revit® design software, for example, leverages thinkstep's GaBi aggregated databases through a custom-built LCA add-on to feed live environmental impact data at multiple stages of the design process.

The architecture firm KieranTimberlake partnered with Autodesk and thinkstep to build Tally. Introduced in 2013 as an LCA add-on tool for architects, Tally lets architects leverage Revit material and quantity data to provide insight into how different building materials and assembly choices perform at various stages of their life cycle. Architects can use Tally in their own iterative digital workflows to back up their claims regarding a design's total embodied carbon footprint or other key environmental impacts.

Phil Bernstein, Autodesk's Vice President for Strategic Industry Relations and a lecturer at Yale University, sees Tally as a good first step in integrating LCA data into architects' workflows. However, because of the abstract nature of the subject, as well as the episodic nature of the workflow across at least a dozen different tools in a small practice and many times that number in some large firms, it is still a challenge for less sophisticated firms, small or large, to take advantage of this data at present.

As workflows shift to more cloud-based integrated data-centric models with a constellation of tools accessing a common data feed, Bernstein predicts a greater number of firms will be able to directly integrate LCA into architectural projects.[3] It is only worth the effort required to understand

Option 1 - Corrugated Shingle Cladding

Option 2 - Translucent Panel Cladding (Selected)

KieranTimberlake, Consortium for Building Energy Innovation, Philadelphia, 2013

Tally report showing life-cycle stage comparisons of two different cladding options. KieranTimberlake's Tally software is designed to integrate into the pre-existing architectural workflow and leverage the intelligence and ease of building information modelling (BIM). Here, two design options straight out of Revit are compared side by side.

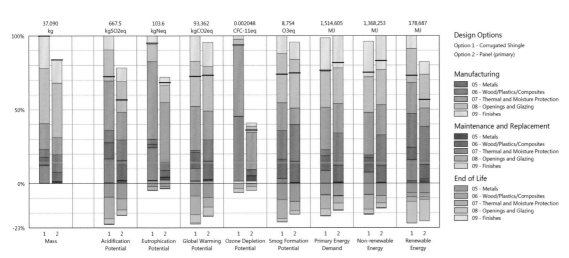

Results Per Life Cycle Stage, Itemised by CSI Division

and technically do so, though, if it produces a significant improvement over current sustainability reporting practices. Architects and their clients are right to scrutinise LCA efficacy and its underlying data quality.[4] There is no value in LCA for design professionals and their clients if it simply creates another costly, more complicated and time-consuming way to 'greenwash' products and projects. Fortunately, evolving LCA practices and resources such as thinkstep's metrics-based sustainable business software, data and consulting services underpin many other high-stakes reporting needs outside the design fields. This broader user-base directly increases the demand for more and better information; the bedrock to trustworthy, data-driven design workflows.

Materiality Drives Trust

'Materiality' in this context refers not to the physical products resulting from the design workflow – the objects, either virtual or real, that are the typical purview of architects. Rather, it refers to the US Supreme Court's definition that governs transparency and disclosure of materially important information about environmental risks

KieranTimberlake,
Consortium for
Building Energy
Innovation,
Philadelphia, 2013

KieranTimberlake used Tally to systematically make the final cladding decision for the Consortium for Building Energy Innovation.

Composite image of interrelated Tally report graphics and data for the Consortium building. Tally leverages established BIM practices to display and use life-cycle assessment data. It provides material information to architectural projects by creating a direct linkage between the Revit model component information and external LCA databases.

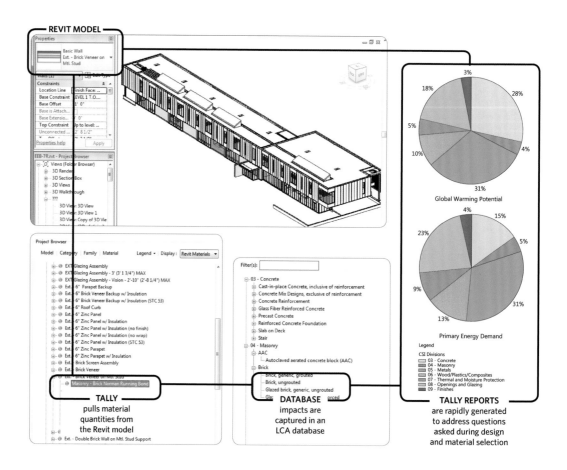

John Cays, Sustainability
Accounting Standards Board (SASB)
goals, New Jersey Institute of
Technology (NJIT), Newark, New
Jersey, 2016

The SASB has adopted LCA evidence-based reporting methods to report material environmental impact information to the public.

SASB
Evidence Based Metrics Goals

FAIR REPRESENTATION
USEFUL
APPLICABLE
COMPARABLE
COMPLETE
VERIFIABLE
ALIGNED
NEUTRAL
DISTRIBUTABLE

deemed critical to guide key financial decisions.[5] LCA data is essential in properly reporting material risks created by any human activity.

'The most valuable currency in financial markets is reliable information,' says the Sustainability Accounting Standards Board (SASB) Chair, Michael Bloomberg, former mayor of New York City and Founder of Bloomberg LP. He explains that the type of financial statistics historically provided to investors no longer offer 'an adequate picture of all that the company does and its future.'[6] The SASB is increasingly pressing public companies to report all material environmental risks to shareholders and the Securities Exchange Commission (SEC), effectively modifying corporate behaviour.

This new, market-driven deterrent to environmentally risky corporate behaviour functions in addition to traditional government-imposed regulatory pressures. Companies are increasingly using ecological auditing services to evaluate and report the net environmental impact of their products and processes, and LCA is already an established standard, evidence-based, method of tracking and reporting this. Separate specialised dashboard tools now provide designers and investors access to the same shared fundamental LCA data sources that support corporate manufacturers' sustainability claims, from individual environmental product declarations to corporate SEC filings.

Materiality underpins the measurable steps business has begun taking to reduce its contribution to human-caused climate change. Those demanding environmentally responsible corporate decisions supported by clear facts can feel secure in the knowledge that companies must, according to new market-driven reporting standards, disclose all material, non-insurable, environmental risks to the SEC. Failure to properly and completely disclose such risks can now result not only in fines, but in a penalty much more effective in modifying corporate behaviour – precipitous share-price drop.

In addition to optimising LCIs for designers, thinkstep provides access to LCA data appropriate for a wide range of business reporting needs. Their GaBi tool provides ecological profiles of individual products; their corporate sustainability reporting tool SoFi builds an overall picture of a company's material risks for investors that conforms to SASB standards. Both draw fundamental

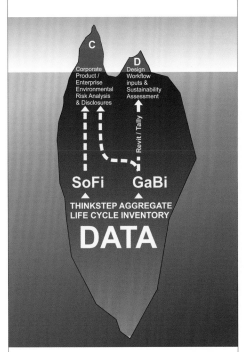

John Cays, Thinkstep core data flow
diagram, New Jersey Institute of
Technology (NJIT), Newark, New Jersey,
2016

Thinkstep, a Germany-based sustainability data aggregator and consultancy firm, provides portals to the same foundational life-cycle inventory (LCI) data for both business and design reporting needs with the goal of reducing environmental and social impact risks in corporate industrial production activities from raw material extraction through to end-of-life.

information from a common database of aggregated LCA source data. Tally connects Revit building information to this same environmental data used to measure and report the material impact of business activity for financial risk mitigation.

Join the Effort

Now that the data and tools are available, our responsibility as designers is to join much larger stakeholder groups – producers, investors, regulators and consumers – in actively reducing environmental risks and continuously evaluating and improving data accuracy measured against empirical reality. New visualisation and analysis tools provide more ways to see risks and control them at the source. Integrating these into our daily workflow safeguards our future as human beings who benefit directly from a healthy planet, and, more immediately, as architects who can provide the evidence-based answers our clients are increasingly demanding. ⌂

Notes
1. For more on the introduction and history of LCA, see Mary Ann Curran (ed), *Life Cycle Assessment Handbook: A Guide for Environmentally Sustainable Products*, John Wiley & Sons and Scrivener Publishing (Hoboken, NJ and Beverley, MA), 2012, pp 1–14.
2. ISO Environmental Management – Life Cycle Assessment: Principles and Framework (ISO 14040), International Standards Organization, Geneva, 2006: www.iso.org/iso/catalogue_detail?csnumber=37456.
3. Phil Bernstein, interview with the author, 29 July 2016.
4. For more information on the current promise and limitations of LCA in buildings, see Katerina Simonen, *Life Cycle Assessment*, Routledge (Abingdon, UK and New York), 2014.
5. See http://www.sasb.org/brandeis/.
6. SASB YouTube feed, September 2014: www.youtube.com/watch?v=qmo5eLbU8AQ.

Coming Full Circle

New Ruralism

Particularly in areas of Africa and Asia, efforts are being made to accommodate new economic development without obliterating the rural way of life. Termed 'New Ruralism', the approach involves architects cooperating closely with local communities, ensuring that projects respect their cultural heritage and empowering them to actively participate in shaping their environment. The process is as important as the form in driving sustainability. Guest-Editor **Richard Garber** explains the principles and illustrates them with a project in China by his own firm GRO Architects, and one in Kenya by his former employers SHoP Architects.

SHoP Architects,
Konza Techno City Pavilion,
Konza,
Kenya,
2012

SHoP was asked to design a masterplan for an approximately 2,025-hectare (5,000-acre) site 60 kilometres (37 miles) south of Nairobi. The local government felt it best to start with a tabula rasa as a way of attracting new businesses to a sustainable city that will be pedestrian centred with live-work programming, avoiding the need to commute to Nairobi.

By using more technologically infused delivery methods that allow novel buildings to be designed and ultimately constructed, an opportunity to bring social capital to such projects has emerged. The notions of knowledge transfer and empowerment of local communities have always existed to some extent in the construction industry – a municipality could, for instance, insist on hiring a certain percentage of a local workforce for the construction of a building. However, since the 1990s – about the same time that advances in technology revolutionised design practice – economic thinkers have increasingly pointed to knowledge transfer as a way of ensuring that information is preserved in the members, tools and workflows of a collective.

When applied to a community, such a process becomes inherently social. In describing this phenomenon, the educational theorist Étienne Wenger has used the term 'communities of practice',[1] suggesting, according to Jefferson David Araújo Sales and Jairo Simião Dornelas, that knowledge transfer has 'the potential to develop intelligence from practical experiences in situations of collectivity and also the exchange of knowledge among its members'.[2] As architects work in increasingly remote places, the opportunity to include social capital as a vital part of architectural workflows not only brings new technologies and capabilities to such areas, but imagines at its core a more integrated relationship between architects, technical consultants and contractors, and also those who will occupy the built projects.

Herein lies the possibility to finally deny the notion that there remains a gap between those who embrace technology and those who have resisted it, in some cases for the better part of 30 years. The latter suggest that architectural design is primarily a social project, that technology serves only in the representation of it, and is therefore separate from its ideation. The point here is not to say that more traditional architects are more socially conscious, but that the perception of differences in matters of aesthetics and social agenda could be seen in some cases as masked by a renewed interest in architectural formalism in the late 1990s. In fact, at that time there was not a robust enough way to examine all of these constraints and criteria in the first, primitive digital workflows.

Through contemporary design and construction workflows, however, this difference can be minimised. Further, buildings designed and constructed during the first wave of these formal explorations – including works by Reiser + Umemoto and those by Greg Lynn, such as his Presbyterian Church of New York in Sunnyside, Queens (1999) – exposed the limits of modelling software at the time, issuing forth the 'digital turn',[3] after which better programs were developed to allow architects and designers to more comprehensively engage, analyse and simulate such challenges. Architects could now virtually investigate how a building design would be constructed and how that construction could be controlled and efficiently managed.

GRO Architects,
Operational diagram
for research
based on knowledge
transfer,
2016

Operational diagram after the work of David Araújo Sales and Jairo Simião Dornelas. Advances in information technology (IT) have revolutionised business practices and given rise to smart collectives – groups of people linked by networked computers working on problems. This is analogous to a shared building information model being developed by different specialists across a design team.

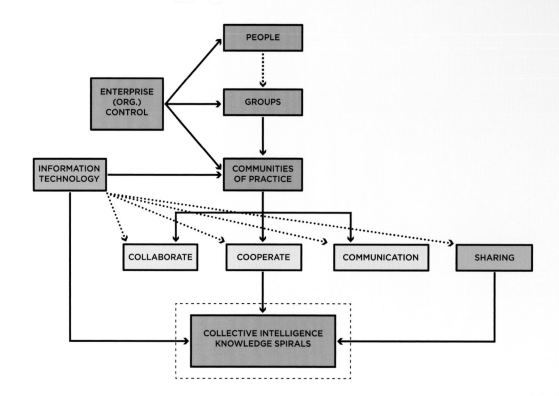

Interoperability and Knowledge Transfer

Interoperability is defined as the 'fundamental characteristic of tools that are designed to work together as part of an integrated system to complete complex tasks'.[4] These tools, or perhaps 'actors', can be simple, mechanistic or even human; each feeding into the expanded notion of workflow designed by architects. Interoperability allows for the expansion of interactions between actors beyond the traditionally narrow design scope of the architect to encompass ideas of information transfer that include direct-to-manufacture components, material procurement, performance metrics and construction scheduling across the team. Throughout the design and development process, a shared modelling environment allows for the analysis of geometry and encoding of metadata that can further control production and cost. This leads to customised workflows that link design data to construction and delivery schemes. Highly quantifiable individual data can be linked to geometry, enabling clients and those who actually use our buildings to better understand how they will interact with them.

The potential here is that the individuals who construct our buildings and those who will eventually use them, each with their own set of biases and needs, can interface with them in their own variable way – a sort of social play on the concept of mass customisation that building information modelling (BIM) and other new design strategies first enabled. Finally, there is a precise corollary between geometry, data and consumer that can ultimately empower an end-user. In prior paradigms, such bespoke, custom solutions were reserved only for those who might afford them. The promise here is that of access to a specific design that can be broadly tailored to larger groups of individuals.

Localised training for groups involved in the production or construction of a project is an obvious form of knowledge transfer. This dates back to the Pre-Renaissance idea of sharing information; however, it is carried out in a way that is inherently scalable – it can be further explained to others via technological means at a much greater scale. In this case, the intrinsic expertise is embedded in the design of the (digital) workflow.

Planning the New Rural

As a planning strategy, New Ruralism is tied to the dedicated economic development of territories outside of urban centres while maintaining, and where possible enhancing, a commitment to both ecology and agricultural production. Stakeholders in such endeavours are often illiterate workers who have traditionally farmed the land for themselves or for larger concerns. A goal of New Ruralism is to provide a better way of life for these stakeholders via sustainable building components while retaining their relationship with the land. In this sense, 'coming full circle' not only suggests expanding opportunities to engage more social aspects of architecture and design while operating in a technological milieu, but also outlines an increasing conviction that an inclusive ecological project can be the purview of architects.

Traditional
Chinese village,
Hubei Province,
China,
2014

Decaying and sprawling structures are being demolished to make way for dense and sustainable communities that allow for additional land to be used for farming.

New Ruralism is tied to the dedicated economic development of territories outside of urban centres while maintaining, and where possible enhancing, a commitment to both ecology and agricultural production.

A goal of New Ruralism is to provide a
better way of life for these stakeholders
via sustainable building components while
retaining their relationship with the land.

SHoP Architects,
Konza Techno City Pavilion,
Konza,
Kenya,
2012

The undulating horizontal roofscape of the pavilion is based on the canopy of the acacia tree – an iconic Kenyan symbol. Shading is of paramount importance on the site, and the roof of the pavilion, just like the canopy of the tree, provides cover from the intense Kenyan sun, while defining the building within the landscape.

SHoP Architects: Konza Techno City Pavilion

New Ruralism as a planning strategy is most recognisably being explored in developing areas in Asia and Africa, where issues of population, agricultural production and ecology are understood as contemporaneous concepts. In such projects, it is critical for the design team to not only engage the programmatic and technical requirements of the project, but develop workflows that involve the local stakeholders who will live and work in these newly planned areas.

The Konza Techno City Pavilion, designed by SHoP in 2012, will be the first facility to be constructed as part of the firm's new 'technology city' in Kenya, the final phase of which is due to be completed in 2030. It demonstrates how SHoP is utilising BIM at a very early stage of project development, as well as digital workflows, to deliver a building that engages hyper-environmental concerns and which will be constructed by a very different workforce.

The technical precision applied in the design of the pavilion, which is essentially an advertising and sales building to attract developers and others to the area, is at some level the same as other projects realised by the firm. However, because in this case it is

SHoP Architects,
Konza Techno City Pavilion,
Konza,
Kenya,
2012

An elevated porch space exists under the canopy, where people can view the developing city and surrounding wildlife. Additionally, the pavilion is programmed with conference facilities including a 150-seat auditorium, exhibition hall and management office.

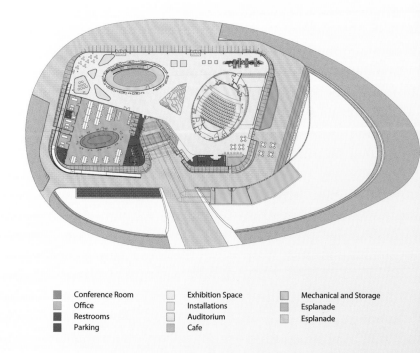

Conference Room	Exhibition Space	Mechanical and Storage
Office	Installations	Esplanade
Restrooms	Auditorium	Esplanade
Parking	Cafe	

SHoP performed daylighting studies to ensure that the porch would be a usable space during the day. The building form is performative, but driven by passive technologies, taking account of prevalent winds and temperatures.

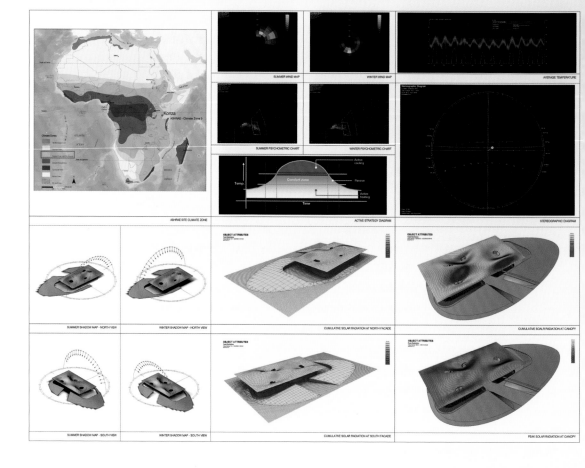

110

SHoP's structural group performed finite element analysis of the pavilion canopy to test for deflection, especially around the apertures that allow sunlight into the spaces below. The same model was then brought into a computer-aided three-dimensional interactive application (CATIA) to produce production drawings of each of the structural components.

the first building in a newly planned area outside of the existing city, the SHoP team operated under a very different set of assumptions and constraints in the project's design and virtual construction. This envisioned a local Kenyan workforce holding varying skill sets to construct the building, with specialised training, facilitating a knowledge transfer of Western construction and technical methods, provided by the local government.

The pavilion canopy is supported by a series of columns that demarcate a series of discrete programmes below, including conference centres and other technology-infused spaces that will ultimately support the research and development that will take place within the city. As shading is important in the Kenyan heat, the roof was designed using Autodesk® Ecotect® Analysis environmental simulation software, and also incorporates a natural daylighting scheme to conserve energy use during the day.

The canopy is made of a notched composite aluminium egg-crate system. SHoP began with a wireframe model that parametrically modulated the apertures, while controlling the structural depth of the beams with finite element analysis software for deflection testing and to codify roof areas that were greater than 900 millimetres (36 inches) deep where heavier

BEAM DEPTH ASSIGNMENT - 36in to 6in

DEFLECTION ANALYSIS

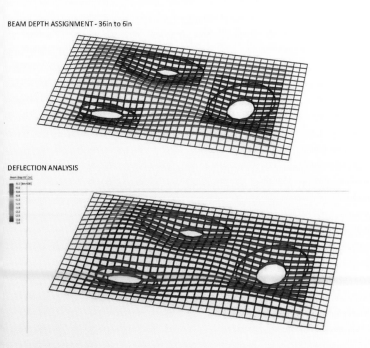

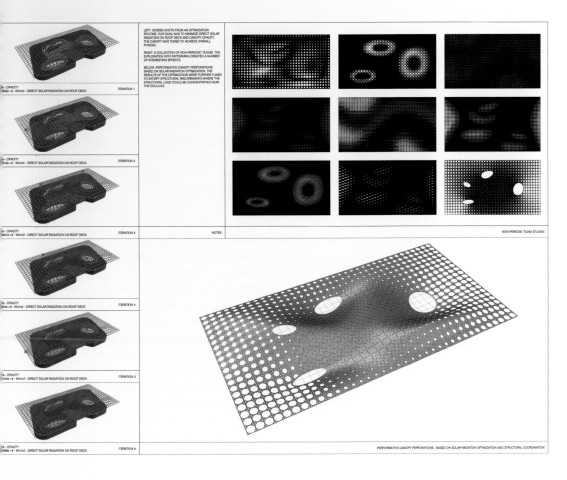

The sedum roof has approximately 560 square metres (6,000 square feet) of walking space and was designed with a series of apertures that allow sunlight through the canopy and down into the spaces below. From a distance, the canopy makes the building appear part of the natural Kenyan landscape.

connections would be required. They were thus able to provide their clients with the required tonnage of aluminium beams and part counts for the roof, as well as details and tonnage of stainless-steel connectors to join the water-jet-cut notched beams, early in the design development stage, well before a fabricator would be engaged in a more conventional design and delivery scheme. The 20,568 unique parts that make up the roof structure were presented to the clients and other stakeholders as a unique kit-of-parts, achievable through fabrication hardware, that could be brought to and operated by the local Kenyans involved in the construction.

GRO Architects: Maozuizhen 2050 Plan
GRO Architects' Maozuizhen 2050 Plan for Hubei Province, China, speaks to a more 'hands-on' empowerment of a countryside community, giving them the opportunity to actively engage in the making of place while understanding the ecological basis of the proposal.

The plan envisions a sustainable yet dense development of housing, civic and educational buildings for the town of Maozuizhen, a rural area with a population of about 40,000, approximately two hours

west of Wuhan, the capital city of the province. Working with the provincial government, and with Professor Zeyuan Qiu and students from the New Jersey Institute of Technology (NJIT), GRO developed a phased masterplan to allow for the construction of housing for agricultural workers on decommissioned farmland. The total land area of the plan is 130 hectares (320 acres) and includes a new government building, theatre, elementary school, community centre and multimodal transit hub. A water treatment facility and recycling centre is planned along the Hannanhe River, a narrow tributary of the Hanshui, which bounds the site to the north.

Density is phased in by amplifying the existing town centre to the north while maintaining open green space that was once farmland and converting it to recreational spaces and parkland to create a kind of green urbanism. The southern portion of the plan envisions worker housing for the farmers who will live in the area and work the land. Here, knowledge transfer will enable the farmers to construct their own highly insulated and sustainable houses after receiving training in construction technology delivered by the design team and local consultants.

GRO Architects,
Maozuizhen 2050 Plan,
Hubei Province,
China,
2012

Aerial view of the Maozuizhen site looking south from the Hannanhe River. Denser housing regions are to the north, while new parklands designed to manage water are located in the central and southern portions of the plan, where building becomes less dense and more of the land is returned to agriculture.

To ensure good insulation, utilising the earth while also accommodating the need for the storage of both animals and farming equipment, a ha-ha strategy was developed to site the rural houses in the southern regions of the plan. The ha-ha consumes the ground floor at the rear of the house, where equipment for farming can be accessed, while receding to the front of the house, where a separate apartment is planned under the main residence that can be entered at ground level.

The planned implementation of better-performing and sustainable structures in rural areas ultimately will have positive consequences on those who live in and use them.

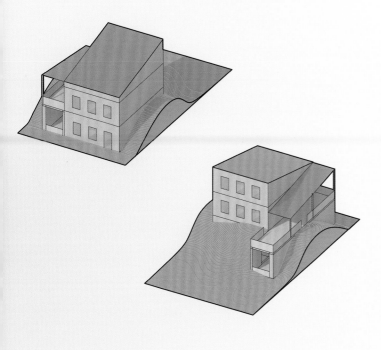

Moving Forward

As the design of new and innovative workflows continues to expand the territory within which architects are able to operate, we have the ability to shape not only the form and organisation of rural and urban communities, but also the manner in which they are produced. The social dimension here will remain challenging, as there is often a desire by stakeholders to retain some of the cultural memory of the old villages that must be mitigated by the contemporary and sustainable advances such projects can bring to a local community's way of life.

The planned implementation of better-performing and sustainable structures in rural areas ultimately will have positive consequences on those who live in and use them. Through knowledge transfer, stakeholders can become involved in the manufacture of building components or construction of their own residences, and in engaging such local contingencies in the design of our workflows, architects will undoubtedly produce healthier buildings and municipalities while allowing for a more collective understanding of how architecture can impact and improve the lives of many. ∆

Notes
1. Étienne Wenger, *Communities of Practice: Learning, Meaning and Identity*, Cambridge University Press (New York), 1998, p 43.
2. Jefferson David Araüjo Sales and Jairo Simião Dornelas, 'The Knowledge Spiral in Communities of Practice: Using Information Technology for Structuring the Collectivized Intelligence', in Carolina Machado and J Paulo Davim (eds), *Transfer and Management of Knowledge*, John Wiley & Sons (Hoboken, NJ), 2014, p 250.
3. Mario Carpo (ed), *The Digital Turn in Architecture 1992–2012*, John Wiley & Sons (Chichester), 2012.
4. Dana K Smith and Michael Tardif, *Building Information Modeling: A Strategic Implementation Guide for Architects, Engineers, Constructors and Real Estate Asset Managers*, John Wiley & Sons (Hoboken, NJ), 2012, p 146.

The southern end of the proposed plan allows for less density than the northern end and thus more organised farmland. As part of the project, the government would lease plots to the farmers who work this land for construction of their own houses.

Richard Garber

Ecological Workflows

Zhangdu Lake Farm, Hubei Province, China

Amid China's snowballing commercial success, feeding and housing the burgeoning population may be a challenge, but it is also a great urbanistic opportunity. With the right approach, it is possible to couple new urban development with land-use practices that are sustainable on both human and environmental levels. Zhangdu Lake Farm ecological village, by GRO Architects in association with the New Jersey Institute of Technology, is a case in point. Guest-Editor and GRO Principal **Richard Garber** describes how a combination of community engagement, digital technologies and green thinking are guiding its evolution.

above: The south site totals 2,268 units with a total gross residential floor area of 368,057 square metres (3.96 million square feet), a floor area ratio (FAR) of 1.35 and a residential site area of 292,200 square metres (3.15 million square feet). It contains hardscapes and waterfront elements with a pervious coverage of about 61 per cent.

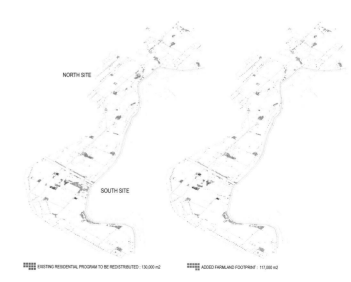

NORTH SITE

SOUTH SITE

EXISTING RESIDENTIAL PROGRAM TO BE REDISTRIBUTED : 130,000 m2   ADDED FARMLAND FOOTPRINT : 117,000 m2

The countryside is inhabited in a more provisional way. It can be defined as a process of 'thinning' – an increase in the area covered alongside a diminishing intensity in its use.

— Rem Koolhaas, 2014[1]

GRO Architects with the Wuhan
Planning and Design Institute

Zhangdu Lake Farm

Hubei Province

China

2014

below: By demolishing existing one- and two-storey residential sprawl and condensing all building on the specified north and south sites, much of the land in the Zhangdu Lake region can be repurposed for agricultural production.

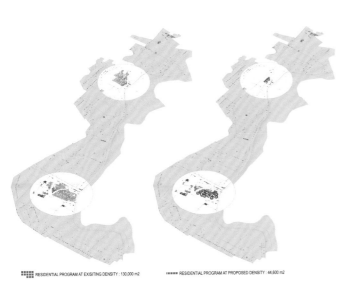

RESIDENTIAL PROGRAM AT EXISITING DENSITY : 130,000 m2   RESIDENTIAL PROGRAM AT PROPOSED DENSITY : 44,600 m2

The seemingly unchecked rapid urbanisation of the Chinese countryside has left many who live in these regions, which currently comprises just under half of the country's 1.373 billion population, weary.[2] Local people, in many instances farmers who have spent their lives connected to the land, do not understand why they are being moved into denser, more disconnected, residential situations as China develops. Meeting the needs, expectations and concerns of those who will ultimately live within these new communities has become of interest to GRO Architects as the practice continues to work both more remotely and at larger scales.

As a pilot project, GRO's Zhangdu Lake Farm plan, executed in colloboration with the New Jersey Institute of Technology (NJIT), seeks to utilise digital technologies in the design and presentation of a large-scale scheme, while also demonstrating to stakeholders that a new approach to workflow can combat the common belief that the Chinese countryside is being recklessly planned.[3] The design process involved extensive community input and collaboration, providing a mechanism by which the way of life of farmland workers and residents could be maintained. Additionally, by imagining a relationship between the proposed buildings and local ecology, the project aims to preserve a sense of nature while expanding the infrastructural capacity of the landscape, which is critical to the cultural history of the rural Chinese countryside and those who would ultimately live in and use the proposed buildings.

The towers on both the northern and southern sites were planned within residential cells to permit an abundance of daylighting and to minimise shadows from adjacent buildings. This allowed GRO to propose building organisations that maximised daylighting while simultaneously ensuring that environmental variables were fully considered.

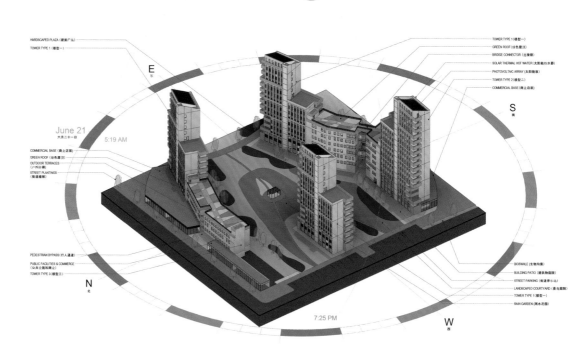

The landscape is a connected and complex system of biodiverse plant communities and stormwater-management infrastructure that responds to existing conditions of climate, vegetation and other geo-biological components. Within the space of the neighborhood cell, the landscape elements transition from bioswales along the very public streets, via grasses, to rain gardens at the semi-public cell interior.

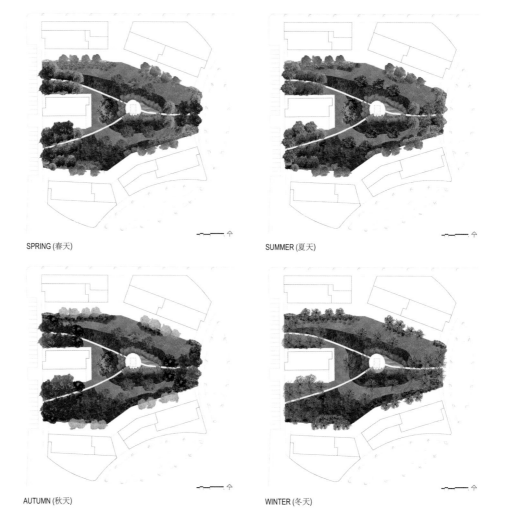

SPRING (春天)

SUMMER (夏天)

AUTUMN (秋天)

WINTER (冬天)

above: The north and south sites, located within an approximately 8-kilometre (5-mile) long tract of rural land designated for GRO's pilot project for a new ecological village. The community will be populated largely by farmers who will work the rest of the land, which will be left for agricultural production.

below: The GRO design team utilised parametric modelling tools to control the size and scale of a series of interrelated geometric components. Once size and orientation were arrived at, the components were developed into neighhbourhood cells.

The (New) Ecological Condition: The New Rural

Some current ecological thinkers make a distinction between space and place, the former being a larger human construct and the latter something that retains not only human, but also non-human effects of things such as weather or climate. GRO's proposals for two new communities within the Zhangdu Lake regions outside of Wuhan focused on amplifying the emerging rural-urban residential interface while being mindful of the ecological basis of the area. The sites, a large south site of 292,000 square metres (3.15 million square feet) and a smaller north site of 113,700 square metres (1.2 million square feet), were selected as an ecological pilot project by the Wuhan Planning and Design Institute (WPDI). For Timothy Morton, 'it is space that has turned out to be the anthropocentric concept ... The ecological era is the revenge of place, but it's not your grandfather's place. This isn't some organic village we find ourselves in.'[4] Such a new community would need to overcome the many functional, environmental and health issues associated with old rural settlements, including the absence of infrastructure, and the inability to manage stormwater runoff as well as water and air pollution, while minimising the environmental footprint of the built environment.

At the start of the project, villagers from the Zhangdu Lake region were invited to complete a survey intended to measure the living standards and quality of services in their existing rural community, and also asked about their expectations for the new plan. It became clear from their responses that protecting the rural environment, and its cultural significance, would be paramount in GRO's proposal, which led the team to explore ecological features such as constructed wetlands and riparian buffers to allow stormwater and wastewater to be filtered naturally and used for groundwater recharge of the surrounding environment.

BOUNDARY

17 "NEIGHBOURHOOD" CELLS
PARAMETRICALLY PACKED

SITING WITH
CANALS

EXISTING AND PROPOSED
STREETS

PUBLIC SQUARES
AND PARKING

RAIN GARDENS AND
BIOSWALES AT THE
INTERIOR OF CELLS

RIPARIAN BUFFER ALONG
SITE PERIMETER

CIVIC BUILDINGS

RESIDENTIAL TOWERS
FAR 1.35

AMENITIES AND PUBLIC
PROGRAMMES AT THE BASE

Neighbourhood – Cluster – Community

The overall design involved the registration of three distinct scales – neighbourhood, cluster and community – in which the combination of architectural, ecological and landscape systems form a new model for rural living.

The loosely organised communities of the agricultural countryside within China often lack the cohesion of the rich social tradition of conventional Chinese villages in more developed areas. Using parametric tools to subdivide and find an appropriate size for each neighbourhood block, and test the potential for social interaction within the given site, a series of seventeen 90-metre (300-foot) diameter neighbourhood cells were developed. These allow for the preservation of existing east–west and north–south roads, while permitting the addition of a series of smaller, 4-metre (13-foot) wide roads that wind around the new neighbourhood cells.

Each neighbourhood cell has approximately 140 residential units that are delivered in a series of both 13- and 17-storey tower types. The towers are organised around the edges of each cell for optimal solar orientation, and are joined by lower, six-storey 'bridge buildings' that contain additional residential units and other amenity spaces such as daycare and gyms. Abundant green spaces between the towers are planned as pedestrian connections to adjacent cells, while also promoting ecological systems, such as the natural drainage of stormwater through rain gardens. These tie into the more robust ecological infrastructure at the cluster scale, where four to five neighbourhoods are grouped for efficient and cost-effective stormwater management and wastewater treatment.

Each of the three proposed residential clusters has a centrally located pumping station accessed from paved areas adjacent to each neighbourhood cell. These transport the

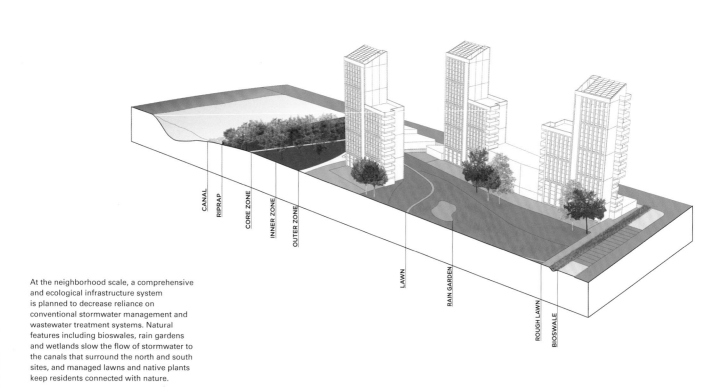

At the neighborhood scale, a comprehensive and ecological infrastructure system is planned to decrease reliance on conventional stormwater management and wastewater treatment systems. Natural features including bioswales, rain gardens and wetlands slow the flow of stormwater to the canals that surround the north and south sites, and managed lawns and native plants keep residents connected with nature.

wastewater collected from the new buildings through a series of pipes under proposed streets to a small-scale distributed wastewater facility that combines both a mechanical system for pre- and primary treatment, and constructed wetlands for secondary treatment prior to replenishing the surrounding agricultural land.

Open spaces and public squares are formed at the intersection of the neighbourhood cells and are coordinated with proposed streets for large gatherings. This ensures the cells are both focused inward to planned green spaces as well as outward to larger, more loosely planned areas for community events.

Groups of clusters form the overall north and south communities. These are mainly residential, but also include limited commercial uses, public facilities and municipal administration, which are housed in the expanded first floors of the towers and bridge buildings along the major streets. Connected buildings, walkable streets, and easy access to interior and exterior natural environments create a warm and shared setting for vibrant community life.

Dense and Sustainable Land Use

The Zhangdu Lake Farm proposal, due to be implemented by 2020, serves as a prototype for responsible development in the Chinese countryside, providing necessary housing for village populations while also demonstrating a commitment to attainable ecological practices. As China continues to develop, and requires more land to feed its growing population, opportunities to design environmentally sound yet necessarily dense communities will continue to arise, allowing the country to urbanise while adopting sustainable land-use practices, unlike many of its 20th-century counterparts in the US. ᴅ

A variable mix of building and ground treatments accommodate storm- and wastewater management schemes, and also ensure that residents understand the relationship of the proposed buildings to the landscaped grounds – an important concern of the local stakeholders involved in the planning process.

Notes
1. 'Rem Koolhaas in the Country', *Icon*, 23 September 2014: www.iconeye.com/architecture/features/item/11031-rem-koolhaas-in-the-country.
2. As of 2015, China's urban population had grown to 55.6 per cent, with an annual rate of change of 3.05 per cent from 2010 to 2015: see www.cia.gov/library/publications/the-world-factbook/fields/2212.html.
3. See Peter Hessler, 'China's Instant Cities', *National Geographic*, June 2007, pp 88–117.
4. Timothy Morton, 'We Have Never Been Displaced', in *Olafur Eliasson: Reality Machines*, Koenig Books (Cologne), 2016 (unnumbered).

Open spaces and public squares are formed at the intersection of the neighbourhood cells and are coordinated with proposed streets for large gatherings.

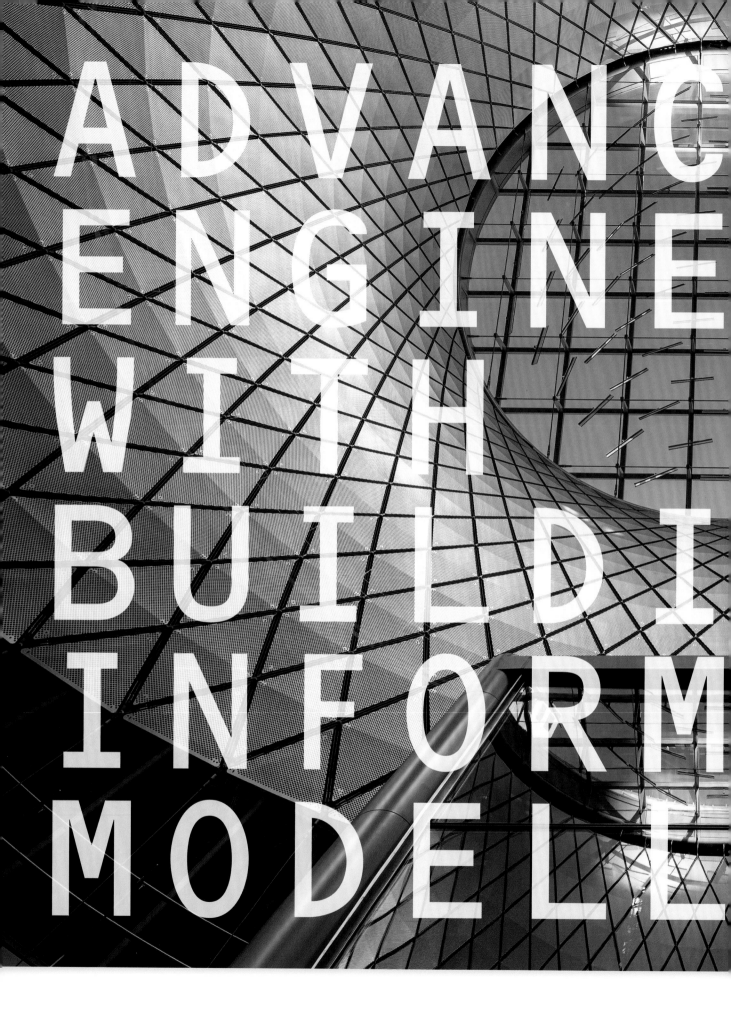

ADVANC
ENGINE
WITH
BUILDI
INFORM
MODELL

Ken Goldup,
Zak Kostura,
Tabitha Tavolaro
and Seth Wolfe

Establishing Flexible Frameworks for the Design and Documentation of Complex Buildings

Grimshaw Architects,
James Carpenter Design Associates and Arup,
Sky Reflector-Net, Fulton Center,
New York,
2014

The scale or complexity of a project can place unique demands on the process of designing and documenting. Successful delivery requires the thoughtful application of BIM tools and techniques in a manner that satisfies the unique constraints of each one, as was done for this project.

Arup is known worldwide for being at the cutting edge of engineering and design development in the built environment. Building information modelling is at the heart of all the firm's projects. As Arup team members **Ken Goldup, Zak Kostura, Tabitha Tavolaro and Seth Wolfe** explain, flexibility is particularly important when establishing a workflow for those that involve complex programmes or irregular geometries: being able to transfer data between platforms can be crucial to optimising the design. Their argument is illustrated by two recent Arup projects in the United States: an airport terminal and a Manhattan subway transit hub.

Building information modelling (BIM) is revolutionising engineering design and the way large, complex projects are delivered. More than just passive containers for facts, building information models are computational tools that can draw connections between different data sets, allowing designers to generate useful new information. The speed and precision with which this information can be generated and shared are changing working methods, allowing project teams, sometimes consisting of various offices around the world, to monitor designs more closely throughout their development.

Workflow
At the heart of BIM is databases holding geometry, spatial characteristics, specifications and other data that can be manipulated to deliver useful information at various stages of design, construction and operation. This information may be used directly or fed into tools that employ it for other purposes, such as quantity take-offs, clash detection, parametric analysis, geometry generation, and even operation and maintenance.

Manipulation and interrogation of the databases behind BIM open up opportunities to not only inform design, guide procurement and aid construction, but also optimise building performance long after the project is completed. For instance, building information models can quickly provide highly accurate estimates of material quantities needed for a given design in the early stages of a project. In the past, this would have been time-consuming to calculate, and the results would have been far less accurate.

The use of BIM, and specifically Revit, has become a normal part of Arup's process and is used on all the firm's projects. In certain scenarios, however, a Revit model is no longer the most efficient method of conveying data. The scale complexity and speed of modern infrastructure projects offer a unique opportunity to push the envelope on the role of BIM, one that is principally focused on documentation of the design. As conventional approaches to modelling and data management begin to break down under the demands of a multidisciplinary design team, opportunities arise to introduce new methods and technologies such as the development of custom-scripted modules and databases for the storage of information. If employed early enough in the design process, these tools can enhance the very act of optimising design, rather than simply documenting it.

Engineers are frequently in search of new ways to store and manage large volumes of design data. For example, when structural element counts become excessive, it is more efficient to both manipulate and convey data in pure database formats outside of the BIM environment. The engineers supplement BIM with tools and scripts used to generate and manage geometries in a rational way at the early stage of design, which can then be imported into Revit and analysis tools.

Dedicated database servers, scripts and programs may be developed to carry out design and information storage of only the relevant data from the results of the analysis packages. This allows for generation and management of geometries and collaboration across the design team, without the limitations imposed by working within one particular tool.

Information is transferred from building information models into analysis programs and back using data scripts, making the analysis more accurate and reducing translation errors. Iterative processes, including design of non-determinate systems such as space frames and gridshells, are well suited to this type of approach.

This process involves utilising multiple software packages to handle and manipulate data in the best environment for the associated task. Software platforms, however, typically have their own unique format and internal processes and, therefore, function might be intractable or not interoperable. Design and analysis software is generally not BIM integrated out-of-the-box and, even when it is, assumptions about engineering or information sharing often do not align with the design teams' requirements. So, while the changes and advantages that BIM brings to the industry are on the whole revolutionising the industry and significant improvements are already being seen, it's often more difficult than expected to fully realise the benefits. Where these aspirations meet technological reality is often where the challenge occurs. It needs to be carefully considered by teams coordinating BIM that the requirements of both full-time and casual users (those not principally responsible for design, coordination and documentation) are met. In addition, the needs of a geographically spread client base often require IT systems and networks to exist locally, resulting in dispersed and possibly duplicated systems.

Arup,
Heat Map informing structural optimisation,
2016

Effective use of building information requires a strategic approach toward storing and conveying it. Here, structural material quantities are visualised spatially to inform conceptual seismic analysis and optimisation of building form. This visualisation came to be known as a 'heat map', and was used to convey many different characteristics of the structure.

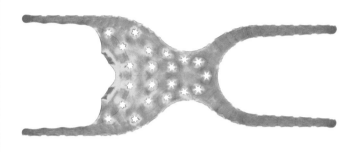

Arup,
WebApp conveying performance characteristics,
2016

Building information is often referred to as metadata, and can facilitate efforts rapidly to explore design options through the use of parametric modelling. Here, relevant performance characteristics are conveyed succinctly in a manner that enables direct comparison with other schemes.

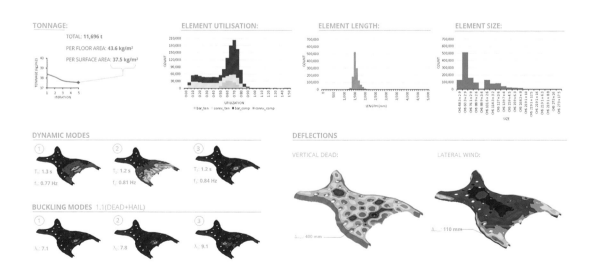

By controlling the
layer parameters
in the geometric
models, the elements
in the analysis
models can be
categorised to
control algorithms
and element design.

Arup,
Structural detail visualisation
using Grasshopper,
2015

above, right and below: Grasshopper
is used to rapidly assemble a detailed
connection configuration for a specified
node of the space-frame roof. The
geometry is synthesised through the use
of general roof characteristics stored in the
project database and a generic catalogue
of specific connection parameters.

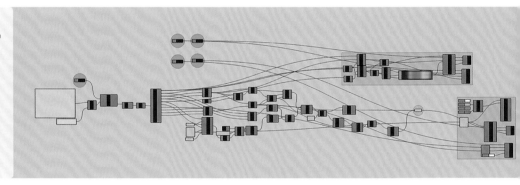

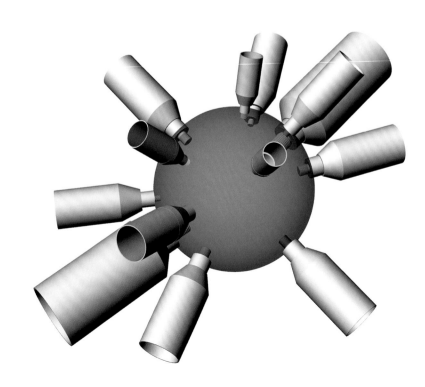

Cloud-based systems that basically centralise data and processing can be the answer. This is not the rule, however, and many BIM and analysis programs, for various reasons, require a local network or local caching.

All of this can result in an IT team becoming 'spread thin' and working at the limits of both physical and financial practical constraints. There may also be other challenges and pressures, such as clients requesting a limit on the geographical spread of their data to match their sovereign boundaries; or from major software vendors with different ideas and directions about how to deliver services and collect fees from their customers. Working with a range of the best tools, creating new ones where needed and realising their limitations ultimately allows the flexibility to do the best work in an efficient way.

Engineering Design and Analysis

Many buildings on which Arup has recently worked have moved towards irregular geometries, either in the external massing or internal volumes, or both. These projects must balance visual interest created by irregular forms with a rational and efficient structural design and repetition in the cladding. The optimisation of geometry at an early stage, when done appropriately, can lead to significant improvements in constructability, and therefore cost and schedule savings, without compromising the vision.

The use of parametric geometric environments in packages such as Rhino3D and Grasshopper creates a setting where centreline geometry is most easily developed and controlled. Rhino provides an environment where geometric algorithms permit the development and manipulation of geometries to inform the geometry of building components. By utilising the integration of script-based tools, procedures can be automated to establish with greater speed the required geometric components to feed into structural analysis packages.

On one flagship project, a new airport terminal building in North America, Arup is providing multidisciplinary design services on a 500,000-square-metre (5.4 million-square-foot), form-found space-frame roof that provides a complete environmental and acoustic envelope for the occupied space within. The architecturally exposed roof system is comprised of well over half-a-million individually sized elements, and directly interfaces with over 30,000 other structural members that provide support for the roof.

It was known by the design team at the onset of the project that the challenge of efficient data management would coexist with ones of a more conventional nature. What was not clear at that time, however, was the specific ways that the design data would be used, manipulated, shared and documented. The design team therefore chose to adopt a framework for storing and managing building information that was truly flexible: one that did not lock project data in a proprietary format, and ensured that it could be translated to other platforms quickly and easily as the right project workflow revealed itself.

At the heart of that framework was the open-source relational database management system MySQL. A centralised project database was established on a high-performance server machine located literally beside the design team. Project engineers, many of whom had never used a database before, had access to basic tutorials and online resources that empowered them with the ability to craft simple SQL commands. Such commands can be used to query information from the server by a team member at their own computer.

Large numbers of team members can access and manipulate the project data simultaneously. With minor tweaks to their SQL commands, they can pull the data in an array of different formats, joining columns of information from disparate tables, grouping information by various characteristics or returning valuable database statistics. A single SQL query can, for example, return, for a given space-frame node, all connected elements, their diameters and lengths, and the forces inherent in each under any specified load case or combination, as determined by the structural analysis file.

The centralised project database is accessed through a wide variety of programs, all inherently equipped to interact with MySQL through the ubiquitous command language. Calculation spreadsheets are developed in Microsoft Excel spreadsheets that are linked directly to the database. A Grasshopper™ plug-in known as Slingshot! is used to pull design data into Grasshopper. It is also used to synthesise metadata that will be sent to the database for storage.

Structural analysis is carried out in a wide range of design packages most suited for the specific task. A range of floor analysis software and 3D finite element packages that rely on a well-structured geometric model was utilised. By controlling the layer parameters in the geometric models, the elements in the analysis models can be categorised to control algorithms and element design.

To engineer the space-frame roof, an iterative optimisation engine using a combination of custom Python scripts and proprietary structural analysis software equipped with a robust application programming interface (API) was developed. A heuristic algorithm drove the selection of element sizes based on a wide range of structural design criteria, material properties and load cases. Iterative information was stored in the centralised database. Updated analysis results easily replaced superseded assumptions in linked calculations, models, diagrams and drawings.

Updated analysis results easily replaced superseded assumptions in linked calculations, models, diagrams and drawings.

Documentation

At the completion of the design and analysis process there is a substantial amount of design information that must be communicated in various forms of documentation. Traditionally, design projects have relied on information shared among team members by means of paper documents. The most conventional and historical way is in the form of 2D drawings (plans, elevations, sections and details) and specifications. Tracking and coordinating all the information contained in the many documents produced for each project has always been a major challenge, and the inevitable misunderstandings and gaps in knowledge that result have led to significant losses of time and money. While producing 2D drawings and specifications is still the most common method of conveying data to owners and contractors, there are additional approaches that can streamline the process depending on the party receiving the information and what the information will be used for.

The successful realisation of Fulton Center (2014), a transit hub in Lower Manhattan that links 11 subway lines, is owed in part to the novel use of numerous BIM techniques. The project consisted of more than seven large contract packages, let to different teams at different times. Fire alarm systems, building gravity and lateral structural assemblies, and building management systems were split by necessity into these packages, yet it was critical for each to perform holistically once the project was complete. The building information model served as the one environment where designers and project managers could view and interrogate the complete design during construction administration. Design changes resulting from field conditions or client direction were updated in the consolidated model to understand impacts on adjacent contract packages. This empowered the project team to tackle coordination items before they became issues for a contractor.

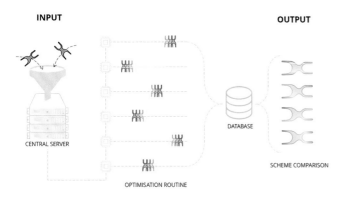

Arup,
Hopper diagram illustrating optimisation approach,
2015

A conceptual illustration of the optimisation approach employed on the space-frame roof project. Custom optimisation scripts and a centralised database enabled the team rapidly to examine and document a wide range of options for the roof form and configuration of the structural assembly. Visualisation tools were used to enable rapid, direct comparisons between various optimisation outcomes.

Arup,
Workflow diagram,
2015

A relational database serves as the heart of a robust and versatile workflow. Data can be transmitted into virtually any format using ubiquitous command languages such as SQL. This allows each team member to build a specific computational approach to a given task, which maximises design efficiency.

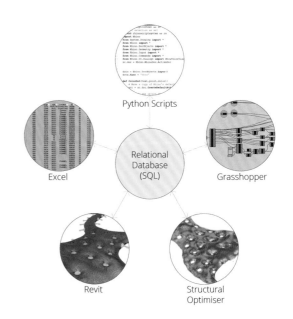

Grimshaw Architects,
James Carpenter Design Associates, and Arup,
Inside the point cloud,
Fulton Center,
New York,
2015

Grimshaw Architects,
James Carpenter Design Associates, and Arup,
Multidisciplinary BIM model,
Fulton Center,
New York,
2010

Isometric rendering of SMEP (structural, mechanical, electrical, plumbing) layers of the transit centre. The model was updated continuously to reflect construction-stage changes in order to identify and address corresponding implications on adjacent contract packages.

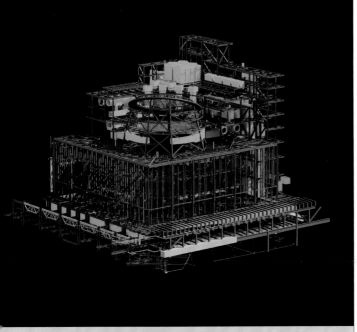

The output of the laser scanning exercise was a three-dimensional point cloud that could be viewed and manipulated in a number of 3D environments. Above, an interior rendering of a scan taken between the installation of the net and subsequent installation of 952 optical aluminium panels. Surrounding structure and mechanical systems can be seen in the point cloud.

At the heart of the project sits an eight-storey form-found sculpture, a result of a design collaboration between Grimshaw Architects, James Carpenter Design Associates and Arup. To ensure that the installation of the sculpture's components and support points met the complex dimensional tolerances required for adequate performance, the building's interior was documented through the use of high-resolution laser scanning at several critical construction milestones. The point clouds generated by this exercise were overlaid with the project building information model to track the progress of installation and control quality of the final product.

Building information models can communicate a large range of information far beyond 3D geometric arrangements. Utilising a database structure, the models can be a repository for a large range of parameters including element materials, connection forces, camber and stud counts, and time-based parameters such as sequence and phasing.

For documentation of the airport project's space-frame roof, design data relevant to the contractor was packaged within the database and exported as a set of concise comma-delimited (csv) files. These files, which documented all relevant structural characteristics of the space-frame roof for construction, amounted to just over 60 megabytes. To interface with the other building systems, we used a set of Autodesk Dynamo and Grasshopper scripts to derive 3D models of the roof system for import into the project Revit model.

Delivery

This flexible framework for developing and documenting design information enabled the design team continually to reinvent the analysis and design workflow as the airport project progressed. It empowered the engineers to assess rapidly the characteristics of a very complex system for the purpose of developing conceptual design solutions. The use of Grasshopper facilitated detailed designs fully informed by the geometric variations across the structure. Rhino3D and Grasshopper, used together, helped visually to convey complex design considerations in a clear and compelling manner. And the inherent advantages of the relational database allowed our developers rapidly to build, operate and troubleshoot custom optimisation scripts that made the efficient design of such a complex piece of infrastructure possible.ᴅ

Text © 2017 John Wiley & Sons Ltd.
Images: pp 120-21 © James Ewing/OTTO; pp 123-7 © Arup

MAD Architects
The Harbin Opera House

Richard Garber

MAD Architects,
Harbin Opera House,
Harbin,
Heilongjiang Province,
China,
2015

The building's exterior references the sinuous landscape of the surrounding area. Its curvilinear facade is composed of smooth white aluminium panels that delineate both edge and surface, allowing the supple form to seem sharp on approach.

Based in Beijing and with offices in Los Angeles and New York City, MAD Architects are leading the way for a new generation of Chinese firms working globally on prestigious cultural projects. They have developed a design process that can be highly responsive to a site and draws on the skills of a multidisciplinary team from the earliest point possible. The story of the opera house they have created for the Chinese city of Harbin is a perfect illustration of this, as Guest-Editor **Richard Garber** explains.

Emerging from surrounding wetlands, the Harbin Opera House was designed as a response to the force and spirit of China's northernmost city's frigid climate and wilderness. The building appears as if it was sculpted to seamlessly blend with the site's nature and the topography.

The procession of space follows a conceptual narrative that transforms visitors into performers. Upon entering the grand lobby, they experience outsized transparent glass walls spanning the space, visually connecting the curvilinear interior with the sinuous facade and exterior plaza.

At MAD Architects, the design process is always initiated through a conceptual charge by founder Ma Yansong. Though trained at Yale at a time when advanced digital tools were heavily used in architecture schools, Yansong prefers to begin with hand sketches, which he feels are more 'honest' representations of his ideas. Three-dimensional modelling is then used by the firm's architects to articulate the concepts Yansong has developed for the project. These explorations are never static, and grow iteratively as additional data informs a project's development. Buildings evolve organically over the course of the design process. From very early in this workflow, MAD integrates specialists from all disciplines, including structural and mechanical engineers to ensure design decisions are feasible. The practice currently has offices in Beijing, New York and Los Angeles, responding to the increasingly wide range of projects and locations in which they are working.

A combination of digital fabrication and traditional craftsmanship yielded the striking grand theatre. Clad in Manchurian ash, the wooden walls encompass the main stage and seating. The panels behind the wood in the lobby and theatre are CNC milled to archive the three-dimensionally modelled form. Local Harbin craftsmen layered fine strips of wood on the fabricated substrate to create an effect analogous to a wooden block that has been gently eroded away by Harbin's climate.

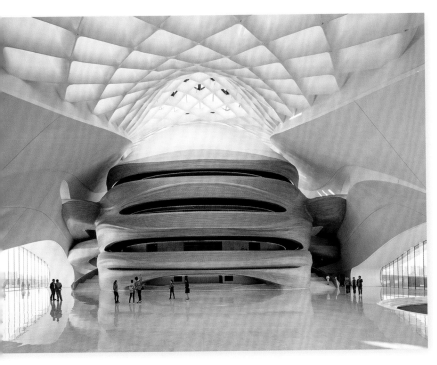

The crystalline curtain wall flies over the grand lobby space and is buttressed by a lightweight diagrid structure. Visitors to the lobby are greeted with warm natural light as they proceed to their seats within the two performance spaces.

A subtle skylight illuminates the grand theatre connecting the audience to the building's surroundings. Made up of glass pyramids, the surface alternates between smooth and faceted, referencing the billowing snow and ice of Harbin's climate.

The genesis of each MAD project is inherently different due to an emphasis on the nature of each place. For the design of the Harbin Opera House in China, completed in 2015, the wetlands and meandering Song Hua River adjacent to the project site heavily influenced its shape and organisation. The design team took from these natural geometries a series of curvilinear lines that give the building its form. The aim was to create a public space, within surrounding parkland, which people from ice-fishermen to ticketholders would interact with – a place for them to visit even when not in the building for a performance. For Ma Yansong: 'From the very start, we wanted to blend the architecture into the surrounding landscape of Harbin, which is a very unique place and climate. We treated the architecture as part of the landscape. It is a place that the public can enjoy.'[1]

'We treated the architecture as part of the landscape.'

Programme and Context

The building's programme is part of a 2-square-kilometre (0.7-square-mile) masterplan for developing the wetlands immediately adjacent to the opera house site. In addition to two concert halls with rehearsal rooms, it includes a hotel and conference centre along with the design of a surrounding wetland park.

Conceptually, the theatres nest within a continuous curvilinear ribbon that winds along Harbin's river-belt landscape. The building was conceived as the conclusion to an experiential procession that begins at the urban scale but also situates its relationship to the surrounding landscape. Upon approach, visitors' perceptions evolve as their spatial understanding of the project's formal organisation begins. This experience deepens inside, with cinematic circulation paths that lead them to their seats within the performance spaces.

The design team utilised a three-dimensional survey to determine the position of each node (x, y, z coordinates) via a point cloud that yielded a series of both digital and physical models, including at 1:100 scale in which the relationship of structure and mesh was explored.

Technical Integration

MAD's design process for the Opera House involved a rigorous effort to ensure that all disciplines came together in a way that would enhance the final outcome. A conscious decision was that the structural 'bones' of the project should be as beautiful and well designed as the architecture. To this end, a number of specialists were required, including landscape architects, lighting consultants, stage engineers, and lighting and signage designers, each working with the architects and engineers to help shape the overall building experience.

For cultural projects that primarily involve the experience of sound, acousticians are critical in influencing the space, volume and materials. At Harbin, a computational acoustic analysis shaped the interior form of the grand theatre, optimising sound reflections and refractions as well as sight lines and viewing angles. By allowing such data to drive the design, the interior becomes a product of the best possible audio and sensory experience for musicians and patrons alike.

The building's complexity required multiple structural systems within its envelope, and thus the input of facade and building information modelling (BIM) specialists early on in the process. MAD's approach to structural integration is adaptive and iterative, where building structure and envelope heavily influence one another. Each of the structural systems

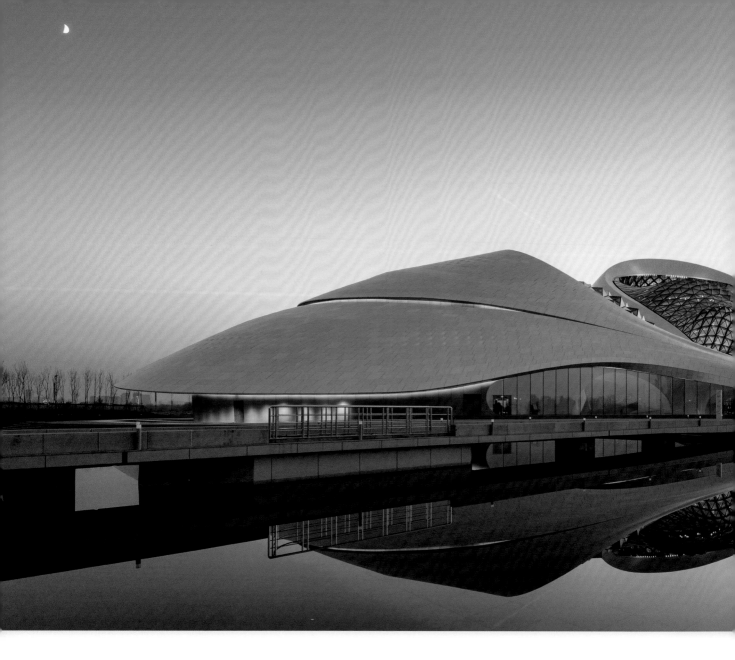

has inherent characteristics and qualities that make them specific to the differing areas of the building. The parking and base building are concrete slab with column and beam construction as this was the most efficient system for the typology. The team integrated a steel radial beam system for back-of-house areas; a spaceframe system for the ribbons, which were required to span large distances without columns; and a diagrid system that exposes itself within the atrium skylights. Though varied, each of the systems was the most appropriate for each geometric and gravitational condition, and the building information model was used both to optimise them individually and to negotiate between them.

The design team worked closely with facade consultants to analyse material appropriateness given the site's environmental conditions. Facade materials were selected following

a rigorous study of environmental impact, performance, constructability, maintenance and aesthetics, with Harbin's extreme temperature fluctuations between summer and winter defining the required resiliency. Geometric computational analyses developed specifically by MAD were shared between consultants in order to optimise facade curvature, define a panellisation schema, and document fabrication and assembly methods.

Workflows and Building Delivery
There were no stops or distinct transitions between building design and construction; MAD continually worked through design-related challenges as they arose throughout the construction process. Central to the firm's workflow is the belief that the best projects achieve a continuity of design from concept to completion, and they play an active role

The Harbin Opera House emphasises public interaction and participation. Both ticketholders and the general public can explore the facade's carved paths and move through the building as if it were an extension of the site's local topography.

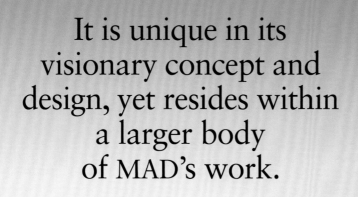

It is unique in its visionary concept and design, yet resides within a larger body of MAD's work.

throughout all phases of the project timeline.

Due to the complexity of the Harbin Opera House, an architect was stationed on site for the last two years of the construction to ensure that the final building met the original concept, working closely with the builders and subcontractors to update any information dictated by field conditions. The completeness of the documentation and 3D building information model helped achieve minimal variation from design intent to construction tolerance. Digital fabrication also played a role in the building construction.

Every architectural project provides vast learning experiences, balancing the knowledge gained from previous building projects with the adaptability that allows for new ideas and methods to arise. Harbin offered many opportunities to learn about urban planning, culture, teamwork, advanced manufacturing,

complex assemblies and, ultimately, the importance and responsibility of creating architecture. It is unique in its visionary concept and design, yet resides within a larger body of MAD's work. As an aggregate of knowledge and experience grown over the course of MAD's history, it will continue to influence current and future projects. 𝐷

Note
1. Email correspondence with the author, 31 October 2016.

Architects at the Mixing Desk

Workflows Cutting Across the Whole-Life Process

Dale Sinclair

Despite the collaborative, holistic approach discussed throughout this ∆, most architects still remain rooted in the concept design stage. **Dale Sinclair** – Director of Technical Practice, Architecture at global engineering firm AECOM and a regular speaker on the future of the built environment industry – argues that several cultural shifts are needed. Not only should architects open themselves up to new building methods that allow them to digitally tweak simulations like a music producer at a mixing desk. They should also make broader use of digital technology to learn from their buildings' longer-term outcomes, and feed this knowledge back into subsequent projects.

Car industry
robotic assembly
line,
2012

Productivity in the
construction industry
has remained static
over the last 30 years.
Will a new generation
of robotic factories help
drive new design-to-
construction workflows
that contribute to
improved productivity?

We are entering a period of seismic change in the way the world works around us. Disruptive technologies driven by technological advancements, generational and political change are core drivers. Architects are not immune to change and it is clear that the transformation from computer-aided design (CAD) to building information modelling (BIM), and onwards to digital ecosystems, will be radically more progressive than the transition from the drawing board to CAD. This is about more than a digital 3D drawing board.

Architect-designed buildings are gaining huge plaudits around the world and clients are very satisfied with the design work, but less so with how such designs are delivered.[1] The expectations of clients are demanding. In an Internet society, clients can obtain knowledge in seconds. When they engage with an architect the bar is high. They know what they want. They know what to expect. Other professions, including lawyers and doctors, are wrestling with similar issues. Professionals can no longer work alongside centuries-old processes. They can no longer base their propositions around face-to-face transactions when Web-based alternatives can now provide instant advice and information. Lawyers are increasingly employing artificial intelligence. The first transatlantic robotic operation, with the surgeon in the US and the patient in France, has taken place. The role of the professional is being disintermediated.

Now is the time to put the creative energy used in the design of our buildings towards the design of new workflows that will address client concerns. As Randy Deutsch states in this $\triangle$, 'practising architecture today requires an equal emphasis on both product and process' (p 58). The articles corralled by the issue's guest-editor Richard Garber are timely. They emphasise the importance of workflows underlining the need to redress the balance between the architect as producer and director.

The Shift from Two Dimensions

For hundreds of years drawings have been the lifeblood of the architect's creative process and the principal means of exchanging information. The articles in this $\triangle$ make it clear that the profession is wrestling with the implications of new technologies in the same way that the art world came to terms with new art forms such as Douglas Gordon's *24 Hour Psycho* (1993) over more traditional forms of painting and sculpting. CAD prolonged the status quo, wrapping around analogue processes. BIM is a game changer. It can be leveraged from the outset. Process becomes integral to creating, developing and progressing the maturity of product. Immersive technologies can better convey design proposals to clients. New software tools allow us to coordinate in 3D as the design is progressively fixed. The death of 2D information is close.

3D printing,
2013

3D printing can be
used for objects large
and small. When will
suppliers allow architects
to mass customise their
products? Can workflows
be aligned to designing
and manufacturing where
larger 3D-printed objects
are printed and assembled
on site?

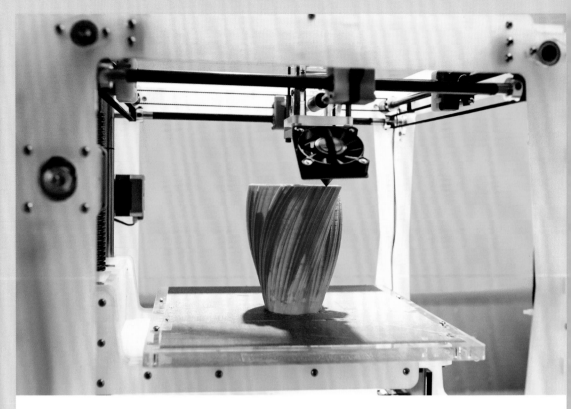

The Beginning of Workflows

Transitioning towards digital workflows has been slow. When we look back we will see the shift from paper-based 2D information for construction to data-rich 3D models used for the whole life of a building as the biggest ever transformation in the way we design. Significant cultural change is required. For centuries we have acted as the architect and lead designer conducting and coordinating the design team from the initial sketch through to the comprehensive set of construction information, assisting the contractor in the construction process. These roles need to adapt to acknowledge the radical changes that are happening around us driven by many new digital opportunities, including how BIM can generate substantial improvements in operational, organisational and societal outcomes well beyond the completion of construction. Do architects want to lead these whole-life processes, or do they intend to stick to the early design stages?

Onwards to Project Ecosystems

The contributors to this issue acknowledge the rapid shift away from simple notions of sharing and storing information to the development of workflows that connect project information more effectively. Examples include automating the connectivity between the architect's 3D geometry and engineering analysis software, allowing quicker, more effective iterations of the design. These new systems are not being driven solely by software developments. Workflows connecting the different software tools together are crucial. Tools being used include relational databases, application programme interfaces (APIs), visual scripting processes, plug-ins, algorithms, optimisation engines, different coding and scripting processes, generative components and feedback from custom computational tools. Most methods are bespoke. They all require new skillsets. They are slowly automating many aspects of the design process.

Those developing project ecosystems that effectively connect geometry, data and analyse is together are sowing the seeds for the future. Game-changing systems that enable real-time iterations of designs are not far away. They will rapidly speed up the design process. They will make it cheaper to design. Such systems will provide the lead designer with immediate feedback from engineering simulations, enabling the design to be tweaked in real time using many different tools. The lead designer's role will be more akin to a music producer at a mixing desk. For example, simultaneously tweaking the wall construction build-up and receiving immediate feedback from environmental analysis software to make sure that the project's environmental outcomes are being achieved, or plugging directly into engineering software to optimise the geometry of cladding panels or structural members. Any pre- or post-production steps that kill the live information in these new digital design ecosystems will have a short shelf life.

We are moving forward to ecosystems where cost, carbon and other data is fed via customised dashboards to design-team members based on instant feedback from analysis software. Digital mock-ups will eliminate the coordination issues typically encountered on site. Workflows will transition from being multidisciplinary to interdisciplinary: a bigger cultural shift than we imagine.

New Design-to-Construction Processes

Stacie Wong's assertion that 'Design is richer when informed by constructability' (p 33) is strange. A core goal of our commissions is to create designs that can be efficiently constructed. Other contributors to the issue allude to notions of digital fabrication, 3D printing technologies and robotic fabrication protocols, but the details around these are scant. The romantic idea of digital construction is encouraging; however, most of the articles focus on design workflows in the concept design stage. Those contemplating radical changes in design-to-construction processes are on the right wavelength. A recent Oxford University study highlights that the majority of construction activity is ripe for computerisation.[2] But before we shift to more radical technologies we need to move away from construction towards assembling buildings on site, making the process faster, safer, cheaper and better environmentally.[3] Simply, traditional construction processes are hard-baked into our current design processes. We must change our design culture radically towards assembling buildings using current technologies before we conceive them for the next digital wave.

Disrupting Design to Construction

A number of contributors point to the importance of specialist subcontractors and fabricators in the design process. Current procurement models reinforce the disconnect between the architect and these crucial designers. No form of procurement has resolved the time, cost and quality conundrums that rotate around the crucial relationship between the design team and the specialist subcontractors. And there is none on the horizon. Construction management (CM) resolves the quality aspect, but has been proven not to deliver on cost. Early Contractor Involvement, or increasingly Innovation (ECI), is seen as a way of effectively connecting every designer together, yet private-sector clients are eschewing this form of procurement, preferring a more direct interface and an ability to exert more influence with the design team in the early stages.

It is inevitable that a disruptor will come along and radically transform how we transition through the design and construction processes. The goal is simple: the process should take weeks not years. We should be delivering 'live' digital design information that seamlessly plugs into digital construction processes, not dead information that is out of date as soon as it is loaded into a common data environment. The notion of the architect hitting the print button to construct a building is not far away.

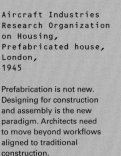

Aircraft Industries Research Organization on Housing, Prefabricated house, London, 1945

Prefabrication is not new. Designing for construction and assembly is the new paradigm. Architects need to move beyond workflows aligned to traditional construction.

Drone copter observing
a construction site,
2016

Refurbishment of and
extensions to existing buildings
are a core source of project
work. Drones are central to
providing the high-quality
information required to
integrate data-rich surveys
into the workflows for these
projects.

Architecture as Art

A number of articles in the issue look at the poetic aspects of architecture as art, setting out notions of design ideas being conceived in remote locations, prepared using technology that redefines old crafts such as sketching, or promotes the continued use of model making. Architecture requires creativity and it is essential that we consider the different means of triggering the creative spark. One solution may be the adoption of new presentation techniques such as photographic images or abstract model making that are conceived as part of new digital workflows.

What is clear is that when architects are defining new workflows that allow the engineering aspects of our designs to be integrated and iterated with unfathomable speed, we also need to pause and consider how these systems engage with our highly individual design processes.

In the longer term traditional design tools will not be effective beyond the generation of the initial idea. It is folly to consider that they will be used deeper into the design process. Perhaps those whose unique design processes can quickly plug into the new project ecosystems will result in the perfect balance between creativity and efficiency. Perhaps those commencing with digital tools will win the day. Only time will tell.

Systemising Knowledge

The processes outlined above require the use and understanding of many different new digital tools. In many respects they are automating analogue ways of designing. They still rely on heuristic methods of passing knowledge down through the generations through learning on the job rather than knowledge being encapsulated in the systems we use. As artificial intelligence, machine learning, big data and other tools that are not detailed by any of the authors mature, our design processes will quickly be systemised, as predicted by Richard and Daniel Susskind.[4]

We need to look to these new ways of capturing knowledge if we are to learn from previous projects and pivot towards design processes that consider the whole life of our buildings as part of circular workflows that feed back learning from our completed projects.

Engaging with Whole-Life Process

Although a number of articles in the issue allude to digital tools being harnessed to promote social interactions at the earliest stages of the design process, it is not clear what these processes might be. Is this harnessing immersive technologies to better convey design proposals? Is it leveraging big data as part of evidence-based design processes?

Although architects are shifting away from traditional design workflows, new workflows gravitate towards the beginning of the design process and are fundamentally about generating a building as an object. It will take another cultural shift to move the majority of architects towards greater focus on the outcomes generated by the buildings they design, and an even greater one to embrace circular whole-life design processes where the lessons learned from buildings in use can be used to inform new briefing processes. At AECOM we are currently developing systems for the Sydney Opera House that will create accurate asset information, and by leveraging BIM-enabled dynamic measurement via smart sensors will improve energy performance and other operational outcomes.

It is encouraging to see architects inventing new workflows. If the architectural profession is to remain relevant in the future these need to evolve beyond the initial design stages to embrace new procurement models, new ways of designing for assembly, whole-life processes and harnessing big data to deliver better client outcomes. There is a lot of innovation and engagement required if we are to continue to play a pivotal role on our projects. How we design will inevitably become as important as what we design. ⚖

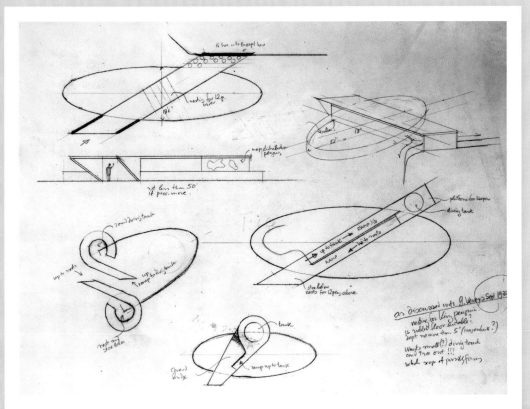

Lubetkin Drake & Tecton,
Early sketches for the
Penguin Pool,
London Zoo,
Regent's Park,
London,
1928

Sketching has always been an important design tool and will continue to be so. In the connected world of geometry, data and analysis, it remains relevant but not core to workflows.

Denys Lasdun & Partners,
Discarded models of the
Royal National Theatre,
South Bank,
London,
1970

As immersive technologies become prevalent, will model-making continue to add value to workflows? This pile of discarded models was referred to by Denys Lasdun as the 'scrapheap'.

Notes
1. *What Clients Think of Architects, Feedback from the 'Working with Architects' Client Survey 2016*, RIBA, 2016: www.architecture.com/RIBA/Professionalsupport/RIBAforclients/RIBAforclients.aspx.
2. Carl Benedikt Frey and Michael A Osborne, *The Future of Employment: How Susceptible are Jobs to Computerisation?*, Oxford Martin School, University of Oxford, 2013.
3. RIBA and Offsite Management School, *RIBA Plan of Work 2013: Designing for Manufacture and Assembly*, 2016: www.offsiteschool.com/DfMA.
4. Richard Susskind and Daniel Susskind, *The Future of the Professions: How Technology Will Transform the Work of Human Experts*, Oxford University Press (Oxford), 2015.

CONTRIBUTORS

 ARCHITECTURAL DESIGN

WORKFLOWS

Kutan Ayata is a founding partner of Young & Ayata in New York City. He is a lecturer at the University of Pennsylvania (UPenn) and an adjunct assistant professor of the Graduate Architecture and Urban Design (GAUD) programme at Pratt Institute where he teaches architecture and urban design studios. He received his Bachelor of Fine Arts in Architecture in 1999 from the Massachusetts College of Art in Boston. He was a fellow at Princeton University School of Architecture where he earned his Master of Architecture degree in 2004 and was a recipient of the Thesis Prize. He is a former recipient of the Young Architects Award from the Architectural League of New York, and in 2016 Young & Ayata was awarded the Design Vanguard Award by Architectural Record.

Sándor Bardóczi is a landscape architect and publicist. He is a guest lecturer and honorary associate professor in the Landscape Architecture faculty at the Corvinus University of Budapest. Since 2007 he has been a writer and editor of *Architectforum*. His publications address the issues of environmental planning and protection, public space and urban planning, and urban and regional policy. He is a board member of the Hungarian Chamber of Architecture's Landscape and Garden Planners' Division.

Shajay Bhooshan is an associate at Zaha Hadid Architects in London where he heads the computation and design group (ZHA CoDe). He is also a studio master in the Architectural Association Design Research Laboratory (AADRL) master's programme. He is an MPhil candidate at the University of Bath, and a Research Fellow at the Institute of Technology in Architecture, ETH Zurich, where he was part of the Block Research Group (BRG). He previously worked in the London office of global architecture firm Populous, and completed his Master's degree at the AADRL in 2006.

John Cays is Associate Dean for Academic Affairs at the College of Architecture and Design, New Jersey Institute of Technology (NJIT). He was responsible for overseeing the development and use of NJIT's digital repository, course management and curricular evaluation system Kepler: A Transparent Coursework Review System. He currently serves as Northeast Director for the Association of Collegiate Schools of Architecture. His teaching and research focuses on the visualisation, adoption and use of quantitative life-cycle assessment methods in the design fields. He is currently writing a book on clearly communicating this technical subject matter to designers and consumers.

Randy Deutsch is Associate Director of Graduate Studies and a Clinical Associate Professor at the University of Illinois at Urbana-Champaign. An architect based in Chicago, he is the author of *BIM and Integrated Design: Strategies for Architectural Practice* (2011), *Data-Driven Design and Construction: 25 Strategies for Capturing, Analyzing and Applying Building Data* (2016) and *Convergence: The Redesign of Design* (Ⓓ Smart series, 2017), all published by John Wiley & Sons. He is a recognised professional thought and practice leader, keynote speaker and recipient of the AIA Young Architect Award – Chicago. He leads an annual executive education programme at Harvard Graduate School of Design (GSD).

Sean A Gallagher is the Director of Sustainable Design at New York practice Diller Scofidio + Renfro. His professional experience ranges from developing land ports of entry for the US to rethinking work–live manufacturing complexes in China. He is Adjunct Faculty at Columbia University's Graduate School of Architecture, Planning, and Preservation (GSAPP) and the NJIT School of Architecture. His work has been recognised with awards from the AIA, US Federal Government and academic community, and has been presented in both national and international exhibitions.

Ken Goldup is an Associate Principal and Manager of Arup's CAD and BIM services, and has been working and developing the use of these tools since Release 9 AutoCAD. He is the Americas representative for Arup global BIM activities, the regional lead for BIM software vendor management, as well as the lead interface between the business and IT team for BIM activities. In addition to a full knowledge of traditional drafting/documentation techniques for all engineering services, his experience includes 3D modelling, structural engineering, object modelling, visualisation, parametric modelling, platform software implementation, and software development from scripts to full programs/databases, user training management and so on.

Anthony Hauck has been involved in architecture, engineering, construction and technology for more than 30 years. As an architect, millwork project manager, software developer and IT director, he has always looked to technology to help solve issues facing the building industry. He joined the Autodesk Revit team in 2007, holding a succession of product management positions in the group until joining Autodesk AEC Generative Design in 2015 as its Director of Product Strategy, where he is responsible for helping define the next generation of building software products and services for the AEC industry.

Ian Keough is the Software Architect for AEC Generative Design at Autodesk. As the founder of the Dynamo project, he has spent a number of years researching how to make computational design accessible to architects and engineers working in BIM. In his current work with Project Fractal, he is developing systems for design option generation and optimisation. Prior to joining Autodesk, he wrote mobile applications for the construction industry at Vela Systems, and worked in architectural practice at Buro Happold Consulting Engineers in New York. He has a bachelor's degree in sculpture from the University of Michigan, and a master's degree in architecture from Parsons School of Architecture.

Péter Kis graduated from the Budapest University of Technology and Economics. He established his first architectural practice in 1997 under the name of Kis Péter Architectural Atelier Ltd. His current office, PLANT – Atelier Peter Kis, has been operating in Budapest since 2011. His early works were mainly concerned with the reconstruction and expansion of historic buildings. A number of his buildings have received international recognition, such as the Piranesi Award for the National Bonsai Collection Pavilion in the Budapest Zoo & Botanical Garden (1998). He has also been the jury president of the Premio Europeo di Architettura Ugo Rivolta award.

Zak Kostura is a structural engineer in Arup's New York office with expertise in high-performance structures. He is currently leading the design of a form-found space-frame roof system for a new international airport terminal in Mexico City. His past work has included tall and supertall structures in the Middle East, Asia and Europe. He led the design of Sky Reflector-Net, a form-found installation at the Fulton Center in Lower Manhattan, as well as the oculus structure above from which it is supported. He is also an adjunct associate professor of architecture at Columbia University GSAPP where he provides a focus on structurally expressive architecture.

Jonathan Mallie serves as a lead principal for Populous. He has met the challenges inherent in a wide range of project types, including sports and entertainment venues in New York and the Midwest, as well as commercial, residential, academic and mixed-use complexes in Miami, Kenya, Botswana, Singapore and India. He has worked together with the leaders and project teams of clients such as Forest City Ratner Companies, Tishman Speyer, Miami Big Block, the Brooklyn Nets, Rock Ventures, Cleveland Cavaliers, Government of Kenya and Google.

David Miller has worked at the highest levels of design both in the UK and abroad, and is passionate about emerging technology, progressive architecture and delivery excellence. Before setting up his practice, David Miller Architects, he worked in the offices of Norman Foster and Santiago Calatrava, then became an associate director of Future Systems, where he was project architect for the Stirling Prize-winning Media Centre at Lord's Cricket Ground (1999). His specialist knowledge of complex buildings evolved into an interest in three-dimensional analysis and computer modelling to enhance building design. This is fundamental to his practice's approach of searching for delight and proportion in solutions to everyday problems.

Adam Modesitt is an assistant professor at NJIT and a principal and founder of Modesitt Design based in New York City. He was previously a project director at SHoP Architects. He has also taught courses on design and technology at Columbia University GSAPP, where he collaborated with the Columbia Building Intelligence Program, and has held positions at Preston Scott Cohen Inc in Cambridge, Massachusetts, and Foster + Partners in London. He holds a BA in physics from Wesleyan University in Middletown, Connecticut, and a Master of Architecture from Harvard University.

Rhett Russo is the design director, with his partner Katrin Mueller-Russo, of interdisciplinary design practice Specific Objects. Their work is situated at the intersection of material behaviour and digital technology, and has been widely exhibited and received numerous international awards. Rhett is an Assistant Professor and the Undergraduate Chair in Architecture at Rensselaer Polytechnic Institute. He is a past recipient of the Young Architects Award from the Architectural League of New York, a former Van Alen Institute Dinkeloo Fellow at the American Academy in Rome, and former resident in architecture at the European Ceramic Workcenter.

Dale Sinclair is AECOM's Director of Technical Practice, Architecture responsible for the Europe, Middle East, India and Africa region. He has delivered many large-scale projects and is passionate about developing innovative, iterative and interdisciplinary design processes. He authored the *BIM Overlay to the RIBA Outline Plan of Work 2007*, and edited the *RIBA Plan of Work 2013*, also authoring supporting publications including *The Guide to Using the RIBA Plan of Work 2013* and *Assembling a Collaborative Project Team*. He is a Construction Industry Council BIM champion, and the RIBA's Ambassador for Collaboration and Technical Advancement. He regularly speaks on digital innovation and on the future of the built environment industry.

Tabitha Tavolaro is an associate principal and design and skills leader at Arup in New York with more than 15 years of experience in coordinated multidisciplinary design. This has included institutional work such as museums, education and performing arts centres in the US, as well as a skills focus on high-rise design in seismic zones, and most specifically in Mexico City. She has led design in a BIM environment for high-rise and large aviation projects for nearly a decade.

Seth Wolfe is a principal and leader of Arup's New Jersey office with over 20 years of experience. He has extensive multidisciplinary design and management experience involving a wide variety of complex buildings and sculptures with a focus on developing structures that enhance a project's architecture through the innovative use of materials and sustainable design. He is also an adjunct assistant professor of architecture at NJIT.

Stacie Wong is a principal at GLUCK+. She holds a BA in architecture from the University of California at Berkeley, and a Master of Architecture from Yale University, both influencing her interest in social architecture and design–build. Named as one of the top 10 most innovative architecture firms by *Fast Company* in 2014, GLUCK+ is recognised for architect-led design–build: single-source responsibility with architects leading the building process. The practice pushes design boundaries with real-world expertise to craft bold and conceptually rigorous architecture.

What is Architectural Design?

Founded in 1930, *Architectural Design* (△) is an influential and prestigious publication. It combines the currency and topicality of a newsstand journal with the rigour and production qualities of a book. With an almost unrivalled reputation worldwide, it is consistently at the forefront of cultural thought and design.

Each title of △ is edited by an invited Guest-Editor, who is an international expert in the field. Renowned for being at the leading edge of design and new technologies, △ also covers themes as diverse as architectural history, the environment, interior design, landscape architecture and urban design.

Provocative and pioneering, △ inspires theoretical, creative and technological advances. It questions the outcome of technical innovations as well as the far-reaching social, cultural and environmental challenges that present themselves today.

For further information on △, subscriptions and purchasing single issues see:

www.architectural-design-magazine.com

Volume 86 No 3
ISBN 978 1118 972465

Volume 86 No 4
ISBN 978 1118 951057

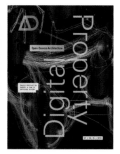
Volume 86 No 5
ISBN 978 1118 954980

Volume 86 No 6
ISBN 978 1119 099581

Volume 87 No 1
ISBN 978 1119 097129

Volume 87 No 2
ISBN 978 1119 162131

Individual backlist issues of △ are available as books for purchase starting at £24.99 / US$39.95

www.wiley.com

How to Subscribe
With 6 issues a year, you can subscribe to △ (either print, online or through the △ App for iPad)

Institutional subscription
£275 / US$516
print or online

Institutional subscription
£330 / US$620
combined print and online

Personal-rate subscription
£128 / US$201
print and iPad access

Student-rate subscription
£84/ US$129
print only

△ App for iPad
6-issue subscription:
£44.99 / US$64.99
Individual issue:
£9.99 / US$13.99

To subscribe to print or online
E: cs-journals@wiley.com

Americas
E: cs-journals@wiley.com
T: +1 781 388 8598
or +1 800 835 6770
(toll free in the USA & Canada)

Europe, Middle East and Africa
E: cs-journals@wiley.com
T: +44 (0) 1865 778315

Asia Pacific
E: cs-journals@wiley.com
T: +65 6511 8000

Japan (for Japanese-speaking support)
E: cs-japan@wiley.com
T: +65 6511 8010
or 005 316 50 480
(toll-free)

Visit our Online Customer Help available in 7 languages at www.wileycustomerhelp.com/ask